How to Pay Off Debt Fast

A 12-Month Plan to Get Rid of Credit Card Debt, Pay Down Loans, and Break the Paycheck-to-Paycheck Cycle

Amy Sheridan

Disclaimer

This isn't financial advice from a licensed professional. It's a guide based on real experience, practical strategies, and what's worked for everyday people fighting their way out of debt. Your money is your responsibility. Before making big financial decisions, talk to a qualified advisor or do your own research.

Results aren't guaranteed. Life happens. Income changes. Emergencies show up. What works for one person might not work for everyone — but doing nothing definitely won't.

This isn't a magic fix. It's a roadmap. You still have to drive.

Acknowledgments

To every person who's ever opened a credit card thinking it would help, and then watched it spiral — this book is for you.

To the readers who are tired, maxed out, and still trying anyway — you're the reason this exists.

Big thanks to the people who shared their stories, their numbers, and their setbacks so this book could be based on real life, not theory. You made it better.

To the friends and mentors who challenged me to finish this project even when life got in the way — I owe you more than coffee.

And to anyone reading this who's still in the fight: you're not alone, you're not broken, and you're not stuck forever.

This is the start of something better.

This is a Bat, Not a Blanket

Let's get something straight right out the gate: this book isn't here to comfort you. It's here to wake you up. It's a bat, not a blanket. Because debt doesn't cuddle you—it strangles you while smiling politely.

You already know what it feels like. That queasy pit in your stomach when your phone buzzes with a "payment due" notification. The internal math you do at the gas pump: "If I fill half the tank, I can still make rent." The way you don't even open your credit card statement anymore—you just make the minimum and pray the balance stops growing like some kind of financial tumor.

It's not just money. It's mental weight. It's lost sleep. It's shame at dinner with friends when someone says, "Let's split the check," and you nod while secretly calculating how much you can overdraft before the bank shuts you down.

Debt is a liar. It tells you it's normal. That everyone lives like this. That you're not really in danger—as long as you don't look too closely. But you're here now. And that means you've already taken the hardest step: you stopped ignoring it.

Now we get loud.

This book isn't some academic report written by a guy who's never missed a bill in his life. This is war strategy from someone who's been broke, stressed, maxed out, and one bad month away from collapse. Someone who fought their way out—not by becoming a monk or winning the lottery—but by getting organized, getting angry, and getting ruthless.

You don't need a PhD in finance. You don't need a six-figure job. You don't even need to be good with money. You just need the right plan, the right mindset, and a timeline that doesn't feel like death by spreadsheet. This book is that.

You can crush your debt in 12 months. Faster than that, even. You can go from barely surviving to watching your balance hit zero and your savings hit four digits. You can breathe again. Sleep again. Say "yes" to dinner without panic.

But it's going to take action. Discipline. And a little bit of rage.

So if you're looking for something soft and soothing, you've got the wrong book. But if you're ready to punch debt in the face and take back your damn life—then welcome. Let's get to work.

The Wake-Up Call You Didn't Want but Needed

Let's not sugarcoat this. If you picked up this book, you're probably in some kind of money hell. Credit cards maxed out, student loans lurking, paycheck gone two days after it hits. And you're sick of pretending everything's fine while quietly panicking every time your phone buzzes with another bill notification.

You're not alone. Millions are in this same boat, rowing hard just to stay in place. The system was built this way—slick ads, "easy" financing, minimum payments that feel manageable but quietly bleed you dry over years. Debt isn't just a math problem. It's a trap. A slow, squeezing pressure that messes with your sleep, your self-worth, and your future.

But here's the twist: getting out isn't about being a genius with spreadsheets or eating rice and beans until you cry. It's about deciding you're done letting this beast control you. That's it. The real shift happens the moment you stop accepting debt as a normal part of life.

This book isn't going to give you empty pep talks or tell you to skip your morning latte like that's the reason you're drowning. That's not only tone-deaf—it's insulting. You're not here because you spent too much on coffee. You're here because life hit hard, or things spiraled, or maybe no one ever showed you what actually works.

Now, you're about to learn.

You'll see exactly what it takes to pay off your credit cards, crush your loans, and breathe again—without having to move into a van or sell your soul. You'll get plans that work in the real world. Tools that work with your brain, not against it. And scripts to use when you're talking to companies that would rather keep you confused and quiet.

You're not broken. You're just stuck in a cycle that rewards delay and punishes momentum. We're breaking that cycle, starting right here.

You're going to feel uncomfortable. You'll probably get pissed off—at the banks, at the system, maybe even at yourself. That's good. That means you're waking up. And a person who's awake is dangerous to a system that relies on your silence.

So take a second and mark this moment. You're not just reading a book. You're making a decision. And that decision is going to change everything.

Let's go.

You're Not Lazy, You're in a System Built to Keep You Broke

If you've ever looked at your bank balance, felt a spike of shame, and thought, "I should have this figured out by now," pause right there. That voice in your head isn't your own. It's the system talking. The one that trains you to believe financial failure is a personal flaw instead of the inevitable result of how things are set up.

Let's get this straight: You're not lazy. You're not stupid. You're not irresponsible. You're playing a rigged game, and no one handed you the rulebook.

Credit cards were designed to get you hooked. Think about it. They offer you a shiny card, a spending limit that feels like free money, and a cheerful minimum payment so low it barely dents the balance. It's a drug dealer model. First hit's easy. After that, good luck getting out.

Same goes for loans. You sign the dotted line for school, a car, maybe a medical bill you didn't ask for, and suddenly you're locked into years of paying interest that stacks up faster than your paycheck. And then they tell you to just "budget better."

That's like blaming the mouse for not escaping the trap.

This system profits from your stress. From your confusion. From your guilt. If they can keep you feeling like the failure, you won't look up long enough to question why your interest rate is 25% while the bank's CEO gets a bonus for screwing you.

You don't fix this by feeling bad. You fix this by getting smart and fighting back. You learn how the game is played so you can beat it.

That starts with letting go of the shame. Because shame keeps you stuck. It makes you hide your statements in a drawer and avoid checking your balances. It whispers, "You're the only one who doesn't get it," when in reality, millions of people are fighting the exact same battle.

This chapter—and this book—isn't about blaming. It's about building. Not some fantasy life where you become a minimalist monk or win the lottery, but a real plan that fits your real life.

Because once you see the system for what it is, you stop blaming yourself and start taking your power back.

And that's when everything starts to change.

What Debt Really Costs You (It's Not Just Money)

People talk about debt like it's just numbers. Like it's just a few balances on a screen or a payment you set on autopay. But if you've lived in debt for any amount of time, you already know—it's not just money. It's mental. It's emotional. It's physical. It changes the way you think, the way you move, the way you see yourself.

Debt is waking up every morning with a low-level buzz of anxiety you can't quite place until you remember that your credit card bill is due Friday and your account balance is already laughable. It's not sleeping well because you're mentally calculating late fees, overdraft charges, and rent. It's snapping at people you love because your brain is so fried from constant financial tension that you can't process one more thing.

It's decision fatigue. It's debating in the grocery store over whether to buy the good coffee or the cheapest option that tastes like regret. It's skipping dinners with friends. Cancelling trips. Pretending you're "just busy" when really, your budget's already tapped out for the month.

Debt shrinks your world. It makes your future feel smaller. It makes everything feel like a maybe instead of a yes. Want to move to a new city? Start a business? Go back to school? Too bad—you've got a $400 payment dragging behind you like a weight around your ankle.

And yeah, it's also expensive. Like, stupid expensive. Credit cards charge interest rates that would make a loan shark blush. That $70 pair of sneakers? If you're just making minimum payments, you could be paying for them for the next 18 months. That $1,500 emergency? By the time it's paid off, it's cost you double. Debt turns every emergency into a long-term financial hangover.

But the real cost? It's the way it erodes your confidence. Slowly. Quietly. It makes you doubt your ability to fix things. Makes you feel behind everyone else. Like you're the only one who missed the memo on adulthood. It messes with your identity. Instead of seeing yourself as capable, smart, and in control—you start to see yourself as someone who just can't get it together.

And look, the financial industry banks on this. They want you overwhelmed. They want you discouraged. Because discouraged people don't push back. They don't negotiate. They don't dig into the fine print. They just keep paying, silently, for years. That's the model. That's how they win.

But not you. Not anymore.

Because the second you start seeing these hidden costs—not just the dollars, but the stress, the delay, the weight—you start to get pissed. And that's good. That fire is useful. That frustration becomes fuel.

You're not going to stay in this cycle. Not because you suddenly became a math genius or a budgeting wizard, but because you're sick of what debt has been taking from you.

This isn't just about getting out of debt. It's about getting your life back.

And we're just getting started.

You've Been Sold the Lie of "Manageable Minimums"

Let's break one of the most dangerous myths you've been fed: that minimum payments are a sign you're doing okay. You're not late, right? You're not in default. You're keeping up. That's got to count for something.

Here's the ugly truth—minimum payments are designed to keep you in debt, not help you out of it. They're the treadmill under your feet. You feel like you're moving, but you're not going anywhere.

Let's say you owe $7,000 on a credit card with a 22% interest rate. If you only pay the minimum—let's say 2.5% of the balance—it'll take you over 20 years to pay it off. And you'll shell out nearly double that original amount in interest alone. So yeah, you paid that $7,000 back... and gave the bank another $7,000 for the privilege. That's not progress. That's financial waterboarding.

The minimum keeps you docile. It feels manageable. You tell yourself you're "on top of it." But you're really just feeding the bank's bonus pool while your own future bleeds out slowly.

And the kicker? The companies behind those cards know exactly what they're doing. Their business model is built on your long-term servitude. They bank—literally—on you sticking with minimums because they know most people won't run the numbers. Most people won't question it. Most people will mistake movement for progress.

So don't beat yourself up for falling for it. The system is slick. The bills are structured to look reasonable. The statements even helpfully suggest the minimum like it's a favor. But now you know. And once you see it, you can't unsee it.

You're going to pay more than the minimum now—not because you suddenly have stacks of extra cash, but because you're done being tricked into financial quicksand. You'll prioritize what matters. You'll move with purpose. And those tiny extra dollars you throw at your debt each month? They're doing more than paying bills. They're ripping apart a lie that's been holding you down for way too long.

Why 12 Months? Because It's Just Enough Time to Change Your Life

A year might not sound like much. Hell, it might sound impossible if you're drowning right now. But 12 months isn't just some nice round number—it's the sweet spot.

Too short, and you don't build real habits. Too long, and you lose steam. A year gives you enough time to shift how you think, how you spend, and how you handle money—without dragging it out so far that you quit halfway through.

And let's be real. A lot can happen in a year. You could stay stuck, spinning in circles, feeling like garbage every time you check your bank account. Or—you could use that same year to completely transform your financial life.

You could go from paycheck-to-paycheck panic to having savings. From juggling debt across six cards to zero balances. From hiding from collectors to calling the shots. That's not fantasy. That's math plus discipline plus fire.

Twelve months isn't about becoming perfect. It's about creating traction. Making moves every single week that compound into something huge. You'll fall off sometimes. You'll have bad days. But the difference is, you'll have a framework now. You'll have momentum. And that's how people win.

This isn't about depriving yourself into misery. It's about creating enough focused pressure that you punch through the wall instead of leaning on it. A sprint with strategy. A season of intensity that leads to a lifetime of freedom.

You're not committing to forever. You're committing to one year. One year to crush your debt, reclaim your brain, and get your damn life back.

You've wasted more time than that doing things that never moved the needle. This? This is the year that does.

The Real Enemy Isn't Debt — It's Delay

Let's be honest. Debt is brutal. But it's not unbeatable. What actually wrecks people isn't the debt itself—it's the waiting. It's the quiet, creeping delay that convinces you to put off dealing with it for just one more month. Then another. Then another. Before you know it, five years have passed and the hole is deeper than ever.

The real enemy is the voice in your head saying, "I'll start next month."

And that voice? It's convincing as hell. It sounds reasonable. It says you've got too much on your plate. It says the timing isn't right. It promises you'll be more prepared later. But "later" is where money problems go to rot.

There's always a reason to wait. A new expense. A job change. A family issue. Life's unpredictable, and that's not your fault—but your response is your responsibility. Every month you wait is another month your interest stacks up, your credit score slides, and your options shrink.

Debt doesn't care about your feelings. It doesn't care how valid your reasons are. It grows while you sleep, while you work, while you procrastinate. It's the roommate that eats your food, messes up your credit, and doesn't pay rent. And if you don't kick it out, it never leaves.

But here's what happens when you stop waiting: everything shifts. That first payment above the minimum? That first call to negotiate a rate? That first honest look at your numbers? Those are tiny acts of rebellion. They might not feel big, but they're how you take back control inch by inch.

Action creates clarity. Momentum kills fear. Once you start, the fog begins to lift. You're not just reacting—you're leading. You stop being the person life happens to, and start becoming the person who makes moves on purpose.

Waiting gives your debt power. Acting takes it back.

This chapter isn't a guilt trip. You've waited because you were overwhelmed, or ashamed, or unsure where to begin. That's normal. But now you've got a path. You've got a system. You've got tools, scripts, and strategies coming your way that actually work. So no more delay. Not because you're suddenly fearless—but because you're tired of what waiting costs you.

The truth? There's no perfect time to start. There's just now.

Right now is messy, yes. But it's also powerful. Because now is when you still have a say in how this story ends. Now is when you can turn the page and write a new chapter—one that doesn't revolve around stress and scarcity, but freedom and forward motion.

Debt doesn't go away when you ignore it. But it does start to die the second you take action. So don't wait for motivation. Don't wait for perfection. You've waited long enough.

Start now. Even if it's ugly. Especially if it's ugly. Because the sooner you move, the faster this all gets better.

And it will get better. Faster than you think.

Meet Your Mess — How to Face the Numbers Without Freaking Out

You can't change what you won't look at. And for a lot of people, debt isn't just a math problem—it's an emotional landmine. That's why so many folks stay stuck: not because they can't add, but because facing the numbers means facing guilt, fear, and years of feeling behind.

This chapter isn't here to guilt you. It's here to get you grounded. You're going to meet your financial mess, not with panic, but with power. No more vague stress. No more silent dread. Just cold, clear facts that you can work with. Because once you see everything in the open, the monster shrinks.

You don't need to fix everything today. You just need to look. That one act alone puts you miles ahead of most people still hiding from their bank app.

Let's get into it.

Print the Damn Statements

Let's rip off the bandage. If you're still dodging your bills like they're cursed objects, it's time to stop. You can't fix what you won't face. And for most people, the scariest part of debt isn't paying it off—it's looking at it.

But here's the thing. Avoidance is expensive. Every unopened email, every ignored statement, every "I'll check it later" moment is costing you money, peace of mind, and momentum. You don't need another budgeting app or YouTube guru. You need a full, brutal, honest picture of what you owe.

So yes—print the damn statements. Pull up every credit card, every loan, every "buy now, pay later" plan you forgot you signed up for. Print them, stack them, and look them in the face like a boss walking into a crime scene. This is your forensic audit. Not to wallow in regret, but to take back control.

This part is going to suck. You'll see balances that make your stomach drop. You'll find charges you forgot about. You might cry. That's okay. What matters is that you stop letting the unknown dictate your next move. Because the only thing worse than debt is mystery debt—the kind that lurks in your mind, inflates your fear, and paralyzes your progress.

You don't have to memorize all the numbers. You don't have to solve it all today. But you do have to know what you're dealing with. That's your starting line. Once it's all in front of you, the fog lifts. And from there, we can make real moves.

This isn't about shame. Shame keeps you hiding. This is about power. And nothing's more powerful than saying, "Alright. Let's see what we've got."

How to Build Your "Oh Sh*t" Spreadsheet

Now that you've got your pile of printed chaos, it's time to turn it into something useful. Enter: the "Oh Sh*t" Spreadsheet. This isn't some fancy accountant tool. It's your personal war map. Simple, gritty, effective.

Open up a spreadsheet. Google Sheets, Excel, whatever. You're not building a work of art—you're building clarity.

Start with columns for the essentials: name of creditor, total balance, interest rate (APR), minimum payment, due date. That's it. You don't need colors or formulas yet. Just facts.

As you fill it in, don't panic. This is data, not judgment. It's not a reflection of your worth—it's a snapshot of where you are right now. And more importantly, it's the launchpad for where you're going.

Once you've listed everything, take a breath. You've done what most people avoid for years. You now have a bird's-eye view of your debt, and that means you can start planning your attack. The numbers might be ugly, but they're honest. And honesty is your new best friend.

You might notice things already: which accounts are bleeding you with high interest, which ones are nearly paid off, which ones are sucking money without moving the needle. That's all gold. Because this spreadsheet isn't just a list—it's a diagnosis. And from here on out, every decision you make will be sharper because of it.

This sheet isn't here to shame you. It's here to free you. To give you a sense of control when everything else feels chaotic. Tape it to your fridge. Check it every Friday. Update it monthly. Whatever keeps it real.

Because what you track, you can fix. And this? This is the beginning of fixing everything.

Why Credit Scores Matter (But Not the Way You Think)

Let's talk credit scores. The magic number everyone obsesses over, the one that supposedly determines your financial worth. You see ads for free credit monitoring, banks luring you with "pre-qualified" offers, and influencers promising hacks to boost your score overnight. It's a whole industry built on three digits. But here's the truth: your credit score matters—just not the way they tell you it does.

It doesn't measure how good you are with money. It doesn't know how many nights you've stayed awake trying to figure out how to make rent. It doesn't care if you're smart, honest, or responsible. It's just an algorithm measuring how useful you are to lenders. That's it. Your credit score is a loyalty score to the debt system.

If you carry a balance, they love you. If you always pay on time but never carry a balance? They're neutral. If you pay off everything and stop using credit altogether? They see you as less profitable, maybe even a risk. So no, your credit score is not your financial GPA. It's a measure of how much profit you generate for banks. Plain and simple.

But—and this is important—it still matters. Not because you owe the system anything, but because the system controls certain gates. Landlords check it. Auto lenders check it. Even some employers check it. So while we're not here to serve the score, we do want to keep it in shape enough to open doors. Think of it like flossing: you don't have to love it, but skipping it can lead to pain down the line.

So let's clear up what actually moves the needle. The biggest chunk of your credit score is payment history. Just pay on time. Even if it's the minimum. That keeps you from late fees and dings. The second biggest piece? Utilization. That means how much of your available credit you're using. Maxed out cards kill your score—even if you've never missed a payment. Get that balance down, and your score goes up.

Forget the hacks. Forget the hype. The best way to raise your score is to pay off your debt and not be late doing it. That's it. You don't need five credit cards. You don't need to open accounts just to have more "available credit." You need progress. And real progress comes from a solid plan, not a shortcut.

Once you start making traction, your score will take care of itself. Will it happen overnight? No. But it will happen faster than you think once you stop feeding the problem. And the beautiful irony is, the more you focus on paying off debt, the more your score improves.

So yeah, credit scores matter. But they're not the point. They're not the goal. Freedom is the goal. Stability is the goal. Peace of mind is the goal. And your credit score? That's just a side effect of you becoming the kind of person who runs their money instead of getting run by it.

The Debt Thermometer Trick (and Why It Works)

Paying off debt can feel like pouring water into a black hole. You send money, and nothing seems to change. Your balance barely moves. The weight doesn't lift. And if you're only looking at the numbers, you might miss all the real progress you're making. It's like trying to lose weight without a mirror or scale. You're putting in the work, but you can't see it. That's where the debt thermometer comes in.

The thermometer isn't just a gimmick—it's a psychological tool. It hijacks your brain's need for visible progress. Because in a world full of bills, fees, and delayed gratification, seeing yourself win—even in small ways—keeps you going when motivation runs dry.

Here's how it works. Take your total debt across all accounts—yes, the whole brutal sum. Draw a vertical thermometer on a piece of paper or print one online. Zero at the bottom. Your total debt at the top. Then break it into chunks—10%, 5%, whatever feels manageable. Every time you pay off a chunk, you color it in. That's it. But what it means is everything.

You're creating visible progress. You're making your effort real. This isn't just "throwing money at debt." This is tracking a journey with a finish line. Every time you fill in a section, you prove to yourself that it's working. That you're not stuck. That you're inching closer to freedom.

Put it somewhere you can't ignore. On your fridge. Behind your bathroom door. Inside your closet. It's not decoration—it's a mission statement. And every mark you make on it is a punch in the face to the system that wants you to believe you can't win.

You can even make multiple thermometers—one for credit cards, one for your car loan, one for student debt. Watch them fall one by one. Watch your energy shift. Because this isn't just a chart. It's a mindset.

You don't need to wait until you're debt-free to feel powerful. You can feel it now. With every box filled, you're proving something bigger: that you're a person who finishes. Who shows up. Who chips away at impossible things and makes them small.

The thermometer works because it speaks to the part of you that needs proof. Proof that this is doable. Proof that the hard days are worth it. Proof that you're not stuck—you're rising.

And once you start seeing progress, you stop giving up. That's the real trick. Not the chart. Not the markers. The belief it builds when your effort finally has a shape you can see.

You Can't Tackle What You Don't Track

Here's a hard truth most people avoid: if you're not tracking your money, you're not in control of it. You might feel like you're "managing" things because you're not getting hit with overdraft fees every other week, or because you kind of know when your bills are due. But there's a difference between surviving and actually steering the ship.

Tracking is where the turnaround starts. Not budgeting, not planning—just watching. Like a scientist collecting data before making any theories. You don't need to fix everything right now. You just need to start paying attention. Because when you track your money, patterns start to emerge. And when you see patterns, you can break them.

Most people have no clue where their money actually goes. They guess. They estimate. They tell themselves little stories like, "I don't spend that much on eating out," or "Amazon's not really a problem for me." Then they look back at the numbers and realize those little leaks have turned into floods. It's not that you're reckless. It's that money is slippery when it's invisible. Tracking makes it visible.

So how do you do it? You don't need a finance degree. You just need a routine. Five minutes a day, or one honest sit-down per week. Pick a system that works for your brain. That could be an app like YNAB or Mint, or just a shared Google Sheet and a few receipts in your wallet. Hell, you could track your spending on sticky notes if that's what keeps you showing up. The method doesn't matter nearly as much as the consistency.

Make it as automatic as brushing your teeth. Every dollar that comes in or goes out, you give it a name. Rent. Groceries. Streaming. Snacks. Parking tickets. All of it. Don't skip the embarrassing stuff. This isn't a highlight reel—it's a reality check. And no one else has to see it. This is for you.

Once you've tracked for even a couple of weeks, you'll start to notice your habits showing themselves. Maybe you're paying for five streaming services you don't use. Maybe your food budget is being eaten alive by takeout. Maybe your subscriptions are quietly draining $150 a month out of your account. You can't cut what you can't see—and now you're seeing everything.

The goal isn't to micromanage every cent forever. The goal is awareness. When you track, you spend with intention. You stop drifting and start choosing. And when things get tight—which they will—you'll know exactly what can go and what needs to stay. That kind of clarity doesn't just reduce stress. It builds confidence.

Because this isn't just about math. It's about identity. You're becoming the kind of person who knows where their money goes. And that kind of person doesn't stay broke for long.

So start tracking. Make it messy. Make it imperfect. Just make it yours. You don't need to be perfect—you just need to pay attention. That alone puts you in a whole new category: someone who's not guessing anymore. Someone who's finally in charge.

Avalanche Vs. Snowball — Pick Your Weapon

Here's where the rubber meets the road. You've faced your debt. You've built your spreadsheet. You've stopped pretending it's not there. Now it's time to actually take it down.

But just like in any good fight, you need the right weapon. And in the world of debt payoff strategies, there are two big ones: the Avalanche and the Snowball. These are the go-to methods people use to crush debt systematically. They both work. They both get results. But they hit different, and you've got to know which one fits you.

This chapter isn't about arguing which one is better. It's about showing you how each one works so you can choose the one that matches your mindset, your money, and your moment. Because the best plan in the world means nothing if it doesn't keep you going when things get tough—and trust me, they will.

What we're doing here isn't just financial. It's psychological. You're not just moving numbers around on a spreadsheet. You're rewiring how you handle pressure. How you handle wins. How you push through boredom and setbacks and the weird guilt that shows up when you start taking control of your life.

There's no perfect method. There's only the one that keeps you moving. So we're going to break them down, side by side. Real math. Real mindset. Real results. And if you find yourself needing a little bit of both? That's valid too. There's a hybrid path, and we'll talk about that.

Debt doesn't die in theory. It dies in motion. This chapter is about helping you choose the kind of motion that'll keep you fired up all year long.

Let's sharpen the blades.

The Avalanche: Highest Interest First, Big Brain Math Move

The Avalanche method is the logical, numbers-driven approach to paying off debt. It's simple in concept and brutal in impact. You take all your debts, find the one with the highest interest rate, and you throw everything you can at it while paying the minimums on the rest. Once the highest-interest debt is gone, you move to the next one. Rinse, repeat, destroy.

Why this works is clear. Interest is the silent killer. It's the thing that inflates your total balance while you're just trying to breathe. A debt at twenty-five percent interest is a financial vampire. It sucks your money slowly and endlessly. The Avalanche doesn't mess around with that. It goes straight for the throat. Knock out the highest interest first and you'll save the most money over time.

This strategy shines on paper. It's the most efficient. It's the fastest in terms of total interest saved. If you're the kind of person who gets fired up by seeing timelines shrink and numbers tighten, this is your lane. It rewards precision and persistence.

But here's the thing. Emotionally, it's not always the easiest ride. If your highest-interest debt also has the highest balance, it could take months before you actually finish paying off your first account. And for some people, that delay in payoff is a motivation killer. They want the win now. They need to feel like something is working. The Avalanche asks you to trust the process even if the rewards come later.

You need patience to ride the Avalanche. Discipline. Focus. The kind of mentality that says, "I don't need quick wins, I want big ones." That's not a bad thing. It just has to match who you are. Because if you lose steam halfway through and quit the plan, the numbers don't matter. You end up stuck, burned out, and right back where you started.

This isn't about being a math genius. It's about knowing how you're wired. The Avalanche is for people who are already fired up and ready to stay consistent. If that's you, great. Get ruthless. Chop down the high-interest monsters and stack your wins over time. But if you're the kind of person who needs to feel progress to stay engaged, there's another method coming that might suit you better. And there's zero shame in that. Because this isn't about being clever. It's about getting free.

And freedom doesn't care how you get there. It just wants you to arrive.

The Snowball: Quick Wins First, Psychology Over Math

The Snowball method is the emotional heavyweight in the debt payoff ring. It doesn't care about math as much as it cares about momentum. If the Avalanche is for spreadsheet warriors, the Snowball is for people who need to feel wins—fast and often—to stay motivated. And honestly? That's most people.

Here's the game: you line up your debts from smallest balance to largest, completely ignoring the interest rates. You pay minimums on everything, but you throw every extra cent you can find at the smallest debt. When that's paid off, you roll that payment into the next smallest. And then the next. And then the next. Like a snowball rolling downhill, you pick up speed with every win.

The math nerds will tell you this isn't "optimal." You might end up paying a little more in interest. But here's the truth those people often miss: math doesn't matter if you quit. The best plan is the one you actually finish. And for many, the Snowball is what keeps the wheels turning.

Because nothing kills shame faster than success. When you pay off that first balance—maybe it's just a store card or a lingering $400 charge—you feel something shift. You get proof that this is working. You get addicted to the feeling of seeing that zero balance. It builds confidence. That confidence builds consistency. And consistency is the key to everything.

There's also a hidden benefit here that people overlook: by knocking out small debts, you're reducing the number of bills in your life. That's fewer due dates, fewer statements, fewer mental tabs open in your brain at all times. Your financial life starts to feel lighter. Cleaner. Calmer. You start believing, "I can actually do this."

And belief is no small thing. Most people in debt don't feel like they're making progress because they never get a win. They're chipping away at huge balances, interest eats the payments, and they don't feel the needle move. The Snowball flips that. You get early wins. You build a rhythm. You gain traction.

And that traction turns into obsession—in the best way. You start looking for extra ways to speed things up. Selling stuff you forgot you owned. Picking up extra shifts. Saying no to things you would've mindlessly spent on before. Not because you're desperate, but because you're hooked on progress.

This method turns the psychological tide. It replaces dread with drive. And that's a powerful shift.

Now, yes, you may pay a little more in interest compared to the Avalanche method. But the tradeoff is often worth it. Because if you stay in the game long enough to finish, you still win. You get out. And that's the whole point.

The Snowball isn't about being perfect. It's about being in motion. It's about doing the thing that actually works for your mindset, not just your calculator. If quick wins are what keep you going, this method is your jam. There's no shame in needing motivation. There's only power in knowing how to spark it.

Which One's Better? Trick Question. The Best One Is the One You'll Stick To

Let's settle this once and for all. Avalanche or Snowball? Which one should you pick? The answer's not found in math formulas or online debates. It's not in someone else's TikTok breakdown or some financial guru's one-size-fits-all system. The right method is the one that makes you move. The one that keeps your butt in the seat and your eyes on the goal.

This isn't a theoretical war. You're not trying to win a debate—you're trying to win your life back. And for that, you need a method that doesn't just sound good but feels good. One that matches how your brain works, how your emotions fluctuate, how you stay engaged when things get hard. Because they will get hard. There will be days when everything sucks. When a bill hits at the wrong time. When you're tired of saying no. When the number on your spreadsheet feels like it's mocking you.

That's when your method matters. Because the right method helps you push through. It helps you keep going even when your energy dips or life throws a wrench in your plan. That's what we're solving for here—not efficiency, but endurance.

If you're someone who needs fast progress and visible success to stay in the game, the Snowball might be your weapon. If seeing numbers shrink and balances disappear fires you up, then build your plan around that. There's zero shame in choosing motivation over optimization. That's just smart self-awareness.

If you're more logic-driven and long-term focused, if you love the idea of saving the most in interest and playing the numbers like a pro, Avalanche could be your move. You might not get that first win right away, but you know the math is working in your favor and that's enough to keep you locked in.

And if you're in between? Then you build your own. Start with a Snowball to get some energy and then switch to Avalanche when you've got the confidence to play the long game. You don't have to marry the first method you try. This isn't a loyalty contest. It's a strategy session. You get to tweak as you go.

What you don't want is to get paralyzed trying to make the "perfect" decision. That's just another form of procrastination dressed up as research. Don't get stuck in theory. You don't need the best method. You need one that gets you moving this week. That's how momentum starts.

Because once you start, everything shifts. You'll see progress, feel lighter, and start reclaiming your power. That's what matters—not how clever your strategy sounds, but how effective it is at keeping your head in the game.

This is about movement, not perfection. Choose the one that gets you moving. You can always adjust. Just don't stand still.

The Hybrid Method (Because Life Ain't Always Clean-Cut)

Some people love neat categories. They want clear-cut answers, a plan to follow, a single strategy to stick with from day one to done. But real life rarely plays along. Sometimes you're halfway through the Avalanche and your motivation tanks. Sometimes the Snowball feels too slow, or you realize that while those little wins are emotionally satisfying, they're not saving you as much money as you hoped. And that's where the Hybrid Method comes in. It's not a third option. It's a mix of both—a flexible, ruthless, momentum-friendly plan you can tweak as you go.

The Hybrid is built for people who want results but also need the journey to feel rewarding. It starts by borrowing the core strength of the Snowball: early wins. You pay off your smallest debt first—even if it's not the one costing you the most in interest—just to get traction. That psychological victory is the gas in the tank. It reminds you that this is possible. It proves that progress is real. And that proof is powerful.

Once you've knocked out that first debt or two, you switch to the Avalanche approach. Now you've got some momentum, and more importantly, you've freed up extra money from those paid-off accounts. That extra cash becomes your financial wrecking ball. You slam it into the highest-interest debt, saving yourself from months or even years of unnecessary interest.

This method adapts to you. You're not stuck in one mode. If things shift—maybe an unexpected bill shows up, or your income changes—you can swing back toward Snowball mode to get a fast emotional win and keep your head in the game. Then, when things stabilize, you pivot back to the Avalanche to finish strong.

You're not failing because you're switching strategies. You're adjusting. That's what smart people do. This isn't a diet you cheat on or a class you flunk. It's a financial mission, and missions evolve. The Hybrid gives you permission to shift without shame.

The best part of this method is that it keeps you engaged. You're never too long without a win. You're never too deep in a math-only grind. And that balance? That's what keeps people from burning out.

You might think this sounds messy. And yeah, it kind of is. But so is life. And this is about finding the version of messy that gets you to zero faster. A plan that feels like it fits your real-world energy and headspace, not some idealized version of yourself that never misses a payment and always has a good month.

The Hybrid works because it removes the pressure to pick the perfect path. It gives you room to win in whatever way works that week, that month, that season. It gives you a plan that evolves with you instead of becoming another rigid system that breaks the moment life gets real.

Debt freedom doesn't care how pretty the process looks. It only cares that you finish. So if the Hybrid helps you do that—take the win and don't look back.

Set It and Forget It? Hell No. Your Plan Needs a Check-In Schedule

One of the biggest lies in personal finance is that once you have a plan, you can put it on autopilot and just coast. That sounds nice, right? Create your budget, set your debt payoff method, and then let it ride like some kind of financial crockpot. Just set it and forget it.

But here's the truth: there is no cruise control when you're in the middle of a financial transformation. You don't "set it and forget it." You set it and adjust constantly. Your life is not static. Neither is your money. Income changes. Expenses pop up. Motivation comes and goes. If you don't check in, you drift. And if you drift, you lose. Fast.

This isn't about obsessing over your spreadsheet every hour. It's about building a rhythm where you check your numbers, your strategy, and your mindset before they drift too far off course. It's like steering a ship. You don't yank the wheel every second, but you don't leave it unattended for days, either.

Set a ritual. Weekly works for most people. Fifteen minutes. Check your accounts. Look at what you paid. Look at what's coming. Ask yourself: Is this working? Is this plan still doable? What's changed since last week? Where did I overspend? Where did I win? You're not judging. You're calibrating. This is course correction, not punishment.

Sometimes you'll realize you can pay a little more than you thought. Sometimes you'll catch a payment due date before it bites you. Sometimes you'll see a surprise expense and decide to shift your focus temporarily. The point isn't perfection. It's control. These check-ins keep your hands on the wheel.

And if weekly feels like too much? Fine. Start with bi-weekly. Or just make sure you always check before payday. But never go more than a month without sitting down and asking, "Is this still working?" Because once a plan stops working and you don't notice, that's when things slide. That's when the late fees sneak in. That's when the discouragement grows.

Also—these check-ins are where you celebrate wins. Did you pay off a card? Mark it. Color your thermometer. Brag a little. Feel it. That emotional lift keeps your brain connected to the process. It reminds you that this isn't just about numbers—it's about freedom. And that freedom gets closer every single time you check in and recommit.

So no, you don't forget the plan. You lead it. You check in. You adapt. And that's what separates the people who try from the people who finish.

You're here to finish. So stay in the driver's seat.

Budget Like a Badass — Without Feeling Broke

Let's be real—most budgets suck. They feel like punishment. Like a parent taking your fun away for your own good. A list of things you're not allowed to do anymore. You sit down, excited to get your money in order, and twenty minutes later, you're sad, bored, and wondering if it's even worth it.

That's the problem with the traditional approach. It treats budgeting like self-flagellation. Like if you just restrict yourself hard enough, long enough, you'll magically fix your money problems. But budgets that feel like diets don't stick. You break them, you feel guilty, and then you give up. That's not how you build anything sustainable.

So this chapter isn't going to tell you to cut out everything fun or track every penny like some money-obsessed robot. It's going to help you build a budget that actually fits your life, your brain, and your goals. One that helps you pay off debt and have a life. Because let's face it—if your budget makes you miserable, you'll abandon it. And if you abandon it, your debt plan goes with it.

The goal is to create a system that gives you power, not shame. That shows you where your money is going and helps you decide if that's where you want it to go. A budget is just a reflection of your choices. When it's done right, it's not restrictive—it's freeing.

Most people live in reaction mode. A paycheck hits, bills go out, a few unplanned expenses pop up, and then they're left wondering where it all went. There's no strategy. No foresight. Just stress. A good budget flips that. It lets you tell your money what to do before it leaves your account. It puts you back in control.

The key is keeping it simple. If you make your budget too complicated, you won't use it. You don't need twenty categories and color-coded graphs. You need a clear, flexible plan that fits your rhythm. One that lets you adjust on the fly without crashing the whole system.

You'll learn how to break down your spending into real-world categories, not just abstract line items. You'll set up a plan that includes actual fun, because burnout kills progress. You'll learn how to plan for irregular expenses—the stuff that always seems to "surprise" you but shouldn't anymore. And you'll set up guardrails so that when life gets chaotic, your plan doesn't fall apart.

You'll also learn how to make this process faster. Most people don't budget because they think it'll take hours every week. It won't. Not the way we're doing it. Once your system is set up, it becomes a quick check-in, not a chore. And the peace of mind it gives you? That's worth more than any dollar amount.

This chapter is where your money finally starts listening to you. No more wondering if you can afford something. No more overdrafting at midnight. No more vague guilt around spending. Just a clear view of where you stand and where you're going next.

Budgeting isn't boring. It's badass. Because when you know where every dollar is going, you stop being the victim of your financial story. You become the author.

And the next few pages? That's where we build the blueprint.

Why Most Budgets Suck (and How to Make One That Doesn't)

Let's call it like it is—most budgets are made by people who either have no real financial pressure or by those who think your life should run like an accounting department. They love formulas, charts, restrictions, and guilt. And the result? You build a plan that looks good on paper and feels awful in real life. That's why it breaks. Not because you're undisciplined, but because it was never designed to work for a human being with cravings, emergencies, and Tuesday-night takeout habits.

Here's what most budgets miss: flexibility. They assume every month is the same. That your spending will never spike, that your emotions won't get involved, that life won't punch you in the gut now and then. They assume you're a robot. But you're not. You're a person. And real budgets have to move with you, not against you.

A good budget doesn't make you feel like a failure. It makes you feel like a boss. It gives you clarity, direction, and confidence. It doesn't punish you for spending—it helps you spend on purpose. That's the shift. You're not building a prison. You're building a strategy.

Start by rejecting the idea that budgeting is about saying "no" all the time. It's not. It's about saying "yes" to the right things. You're not cutting your fun money because fun is bad. You're choosing to fund your freedom instead of feeding the interest monster. That's a win, not a loss.

Another problem with traditional budgets is they rely on willpower. They expect you to constantly resist temptation. But willpower is like a phone battery—it drains. A real budget removes temptation from the equation by planning ahead. It gives every dollar a job before it has a chance to wander off. That's power. That's control. And that's how you stop playing defense with your money.

The reason most people abandon their budgets after a few weeks isn't because they're lazy—it's because their plan doesn't reflect reality. It doesn't include the daily coffee, the last-minute birthday gift, the random craving for sushi. So the second something "unexpected" hits, the whole thing collapses. You feel like you messed up. But it's not you. It's the plan that was broken.

What you need is a plan that fits your actual lifestyle. Something that includes your real spending habits and builds in breathing room. You're not trying to impress a finance coach. You're trying to stay afloat, get out of debt, and maybe still enjoy your life while you do it.

The budget you build after this chapter won't be flawless. It'll be functional. And that's what matters. Because a functional plan you stick to beats a perfect one you quit. Every single time.

The Anti-Boring Budget Framework: 3 Buckets and a Brain

The reason most budgeting systems feel like punishment is because they're built to track, not to lead. They're good at showing you where your money went. Not so great at helping you decide where it should go next. That's why we're throwing out the traditional spreadsheet with twenty-five categories and building something that actually helps you move.

Here's the framework: three core buckets and one simple question—what does my money need to do this month? That's your budget's job. Not to restrict. To assign. You're the CEO. Your money is your team. Every dollar gets a role.

The three buckets are your fixed costs, your flex spending, and your future self. Fixed costs are the essentials: rent, utilities, insurance, car note, groceries—stuff that keeps the lights on and your life moving. Flex spending is everything you control week to week: eating out, coffee, clothes, entertainment, random Target trips. Future self is anything that pays you later: debt payoff, savings, emergency fund, sinking funds, investments. That's it.

At the start of each month—or payday—you look at what's coming in. You drop your dollars into those buckets before they vanish. You don't wait until the end of the month to see what's left. Spoiler: there won't be anything left. Your job is to be proactive, not reactive. Give your money a mission and you stop losing it to impulse and fog.

This isn't a rigid system. It's a living one. Some months your flex bucket might shrink so you can hit a debt goal. Other months you'll have to ease off because life hit hard. That's fine. The buckets move. The balance shifts. The point is, you always know what's happening. No more guessing. No more guilt.

What makes this framework powerful is that it builds in permission. Permission to spend within your limits. Permission to save without guilt. Permission to have fun while still making progress. When you know your fun money is already budgeted for, you enjoy it more. And when you spend from your flex bucket, you're not "messing up"—you're following the plan.

The brain part? That's you. You set the rules. You decide what matters most. You adjust when life throws you something unexpected. Because no one's coming to save you from overdrafting your account at 2 a.m. You have to build the system that keeps your future from falling apart. But now you have a way to do it without feeling like you're living on crumbs.

This framework works because it gives you structure without strangling you. It's fast. It's clear. It's forgiving. And most importantly, it makes your money obey you instead of the other way around.

So yeah, your old budget was boring. But this new one? This one builds freedom.

Scripts to Cancel Subscriptions, Lower Bills, and Get Refunds

Here's the wild part: you're probably bleeding money right now and don't even know it. Not because you're reckless. Not because you're bad with money. But because you're on autopilot. And the companies that charge you? They're counting on it. They bank on you being too busy, too tired, or too overwhelmed to notice that you're paying for stuff you don't use, overpaying for services that should be cheaper, or just accepting whatever number shows up on your bill.

It's time to change that. This section is about offense. You're not just budgeting your money anymore. You're going after what's yours. You're clawing back cash that should have never left your account in the first place. And the way you do it? With your voice. A few short conversations. A couple of emails. Some simple phrases that put you back in the driver's seat.

Let's start with subscriptions. You've probably got a few you forgot about. Streaming platforms you barely use. Fitness apps you swore you'd open. Newsletters charging you ten bucks a month for content you could find for free. It's not just about cutting costs—it's about cutting dead weight.

Here's your script when calling or emailing to cancel:

"Hi, I noticed I'm still being billed for [service]. I'd like to cancel immediately and confirm I won't be charged again. Please send written confirmation. Thanks."

That's it. No apologies. No explanations. Just clarity and closure. If they offer you a deal to stay, say no—unless it's something you actively want and have already planned for in your budget.

Now let's talk bills. Internet, phone, insurance—these companies are surprisingly negotiable. But only if you ask. If you've been a customer for more than six months, you've got leverage. Call them up and say:

"I've been a loyal customer, but my bill's too high. I need to lower it. What can you do for me?"

Then shut up and wait. Don't fill the silence. Let them scramble. A lot of the time, they'll offer you a discount, a promo, or a downgrade that still gives you what you need for less.

And if they don't? Be ready to walk. You don't owe loyalty to a company that's overcharging you.

Refunds are another gold mine. Got charged twice for something? Product showed up damaged? Late delivery? Call or email. Companies are way more flexible than they pretend to be.

Try this:

"Hi, I received [product/service], but there was an issue. I'd like a refund or credit. Please let me know the next steps."

No need to rage. Just be direct. Most of the time, they'll give you something just to keep you quiet and move on. You're not being difficult—you're being responsible.

The money you save from these scripts isn't just pocket change. It's another debt payment. Another week of groceries. Another shot at breathing room. Don't leave that cash on the table.

And more than the money, you're building a new muscle—the one that speaks up. The one that doesn't accept what's handed to you. The one that knows your voice has value. That's not just useful in finance. That's life-changing.

How to Feed Yourself for $40 a Week Without Crying

Grocery spending is the budget killer no one wants to talk about. You think you're doing okay, and then boom—one "quick" trip to the store turns into eighty dollars, and you still don't have anything to make an actual meal. You're not alone. This happens to almost everyone. Because grocery stores are built to drain you. The layout, the lighting, the impulse aisles—it's a trap. And if you walk in without a plan, your money gets eaten before your food does.

But feeding yourself on a tight budget doesn't have to mean eating like a college freshman. You don't need to survive on ramen and sadness. You just need a strategy. One that's realistic, repeatable, and doesn't make you feel like your life is on pause.

Start with this mindset: food is fuel, not flair. When you're in debt payoff mode, your meals don't have to impress anyone. They just need to be filling, cheap, and easy to prep. You're not trying to win Top Chef. You're trying to win your freedom back.

The key is meal planning that doesn't feel like a second job. Pick three to five go-to meals you can repeat. Stuff that uses overlapping ingredients so you're not buying a thousand different things each week. Think rice, beans, pasta, eggs, frozen vegetables, tortillas, oats, peanut butter, canned tuna, rotisserie chicken, bulk ground beef. These are the unsung heroes of the broke-but-winning kitchen.

Cook in batches. Make chili, soup, or stir fry that lasts you multiple meals. Leftovers aren't boring—they're efficient. Freeze what you don't use. Use the same base ingredients in different ways to avoid burnout. Chicken tacos on Monday. Chicken stir fry on Tuesday. Chicken soup on Wednesday. You get the idea.

Also—skip the fancy health trends for now. You don't need chia seeds, quinoa, or organic imported matcha. You need calories, protein, and fiber. You can eat healthy-ish without breaking your budget. And if that means frozen over fresh sometimes? Cool. You're not failing. You're adapting.

Avoid the "snack trap." That's where the real money disappears. Chips, soda, protein bars, single-serve anything—it adds up fast and fills you up for about ten minutes. Instead, spend on ingredients, not items. The fewer logos in your cart, the cheaper it's going to be.

And don't shop hungry. Ever. You will absolutely buy more, and most of it will be stuff that doesn't line up with your plan. Eat first, then shop with a list. Stick to the list like your life depends on it—because your budget does.

With the right mindset, $40 a week isn't deprivation. It's domination. You're proving that you can survive, thrive, and take control of your finances without starving, sulking, or spiraling.

You're not on a diet. You're on a mission. And every dollar you don't spend on groceries is a dollar you use to buy your freedom.

Zero-Based Budgeting: Every Dollar Gets a Job

This is the point in your money journey where you stop letting dollars drift. No more mystery leaks. No more forgetting where the hell your paycheck went by week two. Zero-based budgeting isn't a trend or a theory—it's a system that forces you to pay attention. And when you pay attention, your money starts doing what it's told.

Zero-based budgeting means you give every single dollar a job. Not most of them. Not the ones you remember. All of them. If you make $3,000 this month, you assign all $3,000 somewhere. Bills, food, gas, debt, savings, even fun money—it all gets named. Nothing gets to just sit there. No "extra." No cushion that quietly disappears on snacks and late-night Amazon scrolls. Every dollar is accounted for before it lands.

Why does this work? Because money is like water—it flows wherever there's space. If you don't give it structure, it seeps out. A subscription here. An impulse buy there. Before you know it, half your paycheck is gone and you've got nothing to show for it but stress. Zero-based budgeting plugs the holes. It makes you the one steering, not reacting.

But let's clear up a myth right now: this doesn't mean you spend every dollar you make. You're not draining your account to zero. You're giving your money assignments. If you've got $200 going to savings, that money has a job. If you're paying off $500 in debt, that's a job. If $40 is for tacos and wine on Friday night? That's still a job. The goal is clarity, not austerity.

This method forces you to look your financial life in the face. You can't ignore bad habits when you're building a zero-based budget. The truth shows up in real time. You'll see exactly how much is going to things that don't matter—and that moment? That's where real change begins. Because once you see the problem, you can fix it.

Let's say you make $2,500 a month. Start by listing your essentials: rent, food, transportation, utilities. Then add debt payments. Then savings. Then whatever else is important to you. If you get to the end and you've only assigned $2,200, you don't stop there. You go back and tell those remaining $300 where to go. Maybe an extra payment on your highest-interest card. Maybe a stash for an upcoming car repair. Maybe boosting your emergency fund. You don't leave it unclaimed. Because unclaimed money is always spent.

The first month doing this will feel clunky. You'll miss things. You'll underestimate one category and overspend in another. That's fine. Adjust. Learn. Budgeting isn't a test—it's a tool. And it's supposed to get better every time you use it. The win is in the repetition.

Zero-based budgeting also shifts your relationship with "leftover" money. There's no such thing anymore. If you have money left over at the end of the month, that's just unassigned income. It doesn't mean "go wild." It means you didn't finish your plan. Put it somewhere on purpose. That's the difference between broke people who stay broke and broke people who get out. Intentionality.

You don't need a fancy app to do this. A notebook works. A spreadsheet works. A napkin and a pen work. What matters is the mindset: nothing is random. Everything has a name. When your money knows its job, it stops disappearing.

This is how you stop losing ground. This is how you start making real, visible progress. This is how broke people become rich—with discipline, consistency, and zero guessing. Zero-based isn't sexy. It's serious. And serious gets you free.

Talk Your Way Out — Negotiation Hacks for Lowering Payments

Debt doesn't always have to be paid in full. At least not the way they want you to believe. One of the most underused tools in your arsenal is your voice. Not your money. Not your hustle. Your voice. The way you talk to creditors, lenders, customer service reps, and collections agents can literally save you thousands of dollars and months of stress. But most people never even try. Why? Because they're scared, ashamed, or convinced it won't work.

Here's the truth: it does work. The game is rigged in favor of people who speak up. The quiet ones? They pay full price, full interest, full pain. The ones who push back, ask questions, and negotiate? They get discounts, payment plans, lower rates, waived fees. All because they picked up the phone and said the right words.

That's what this chapter is about. This isn't about confrontation. You're not going to war with your credit card company. You're walking in with calm confidence, with scripts and leverage and clarity. You're walking in like a person who knows their worth and knows the system is flexible—because it is.

Creditors don't advertise this, but they absolutely have the power to adjust your terms. They have retention departments trained to keep you from walking. They have programs for financial hardship, internal codes for interest reductions, hidden tiers of payment plans. But they're not going to offer them unless you ask.

This starts with mindset. You're not calling to beg. You're calling to negotiate. That's a very different energy. You are a paying customer. You're taking responsibility. You're asking for a solution, not a bailout. This works especially well when you've made regular payments but are overwhelmed by high interest or a temporary setback.

Let's say you're calling your credit card company. Start here: "Hi, I'm trying to get control of my debt and I need to lower my interest rate. I've been a customer for [X] years, and I'd really appreciate your help. What options do you have for someone in my situation?"

Then wait. Let them respond. Silence is your weapon. Don't fill the air. Let the rep do their job. They'll often transfer you to someone else who can help—because the first line rep usually can't. That's fine. Keep asking. Keep calm.

Sometimes you'll hear no. That's okay. You hang up and call again tomorrow. Different rep, different outcome. Persistence matters.

Let's say you've already missed payments and you're dealing with collections. This is where most people freeze. But here's what you need to know: debt collectors buy your debt for pennies. They're making money even if you pay a fraction of the balance. That means you can settle.

Start by asking them to validate the debt. Don't acknowledge anything until they prove you owe it. If they do, say something like: "I'm not in a position to pay the full amount, but I want to resolve this. I can pay [X] in a lump sum if we can settle this account in full. Can you send that in writing?"

Always get it in writing. Never send money based on a phone call. If they agree to settle for less, make sure it says "settled in full" on the paperwork. That protects you later.

And if they try to scare you? Stay calm. You have rights. You don't have to deal with harassment. You can request communication in writing only. You can block calls. You can negotiate on your terms.

Every conversation you have is a step toward freedom. It might feel awkward. It might feel uncomfortable. But on the other side of that discomfort is relief, leverage, and progress. You're not powerless. You've got tools. You've got words. And now, you've got a plan.

So let's start talking.

Credit Card Companies Are Not Your Friends, but They Are Negotiable

If you've ever gotten a shiny new credit card in the mail and felt a weird little buzz, you're not alone. The packaging is slick. The welcome email is upbeat. They give you a limit that feels like found money and throw in phrases like "loyal customer" and "exclusive offer" to butter you up. It's all very friendly—until you start struggling. Then the tone changes. Fast.

Credit card companies are not your friends. They are not here to help you win. They're banks. Their job is to make money. And they make a lot of it off people who are just trying to keep up. The longer you carry a balance, the more you pay in interest. The longer you stay stuck, the more profitable you are to them.

But here's the twist: they're still negotiable. The rates they give you are not set in stone. The fees they charge you are not always final. And the limits they place on your options are not fixed laws of the universe. They have leeway—they just don't advertise it.

You have to ask.

And you don't ask like someone begging for scraps. You ask like a customer with power. Because that's what you are. You're not asking for charity. You're asking them to keep you around. And they want that more than they let on.

If you've been making on-time payments, that's leverage. If you've been with them for years, that's leverage. If your balance is high and they're earning massive interest off you, that's leverage too—because it means losing you hurts them more than helping you.

When you call, speak calmly and confidently. You're not emotional. You're strategic. Try something like, "I'd like to lower my interest rate. I've been a good customer and I'm trying to get ahead. What can you offer?"

They may put you on hold. They may transfer you. Stay patient. Ask again. If they say no, ask for a supervisor. If they still say no, hang up and call again another day. Different rep, different results. This isn't about luck. It's about persistence.

Sometimes just the act of calling and asking gets you a temporary reduction, or a promotional rate, or waived fees. Other times, it opens the door to longer-term solutions like hardship programs. These are quiet little programs that only show up when people ask the right questions. You'd be shocked at what's on the table if you just make the call.

The truth is, they don't want you to default. That costs them money. They want to keep you paying. So if lowering your interest helps you do that, they'll often say yes.

Will every company work with you? No. But many will. And even one lower rate can save you hundreds—or thousands—over time. That's real money. That's faster progress. That's one less barrier between you and freedom.

Don't let a company's friendliness trick you into staying quiet. This is a business. So treat it like one. And go get your discount.

Word-for-Word Script to Lower Your Interest Rate Today

It's easy to tell someone, "Just call your credit card company and ask for a better rate." But what exactly do you say when they answer? What if your voice shakes? What if they push back? What if you freeze up mid-call and hang up with nothing to show for it?

That's where a script comes in. Not because you're weak, but because you're prepared. Having the words in front of you is like having a safety net. You know your lines. You know your goal. You sound like someone who knows what they're doing—even if you're sweating through your shirt.

Here's the baseline call structure. Practice it once or twice out loud. Then dial.

"Hi, I'm calling because I want to lower my credit card's interest rate. I've been a customer for [insert number] years, I've been making payments on time, and I'm working on paying down my balance. I'd really appreciate it if you could help me out. What options do you have for reducing my APR?"

Then stop talking. Seriously. Stop. Let the rep respond. They might offer you a temporary promotional rate. They might say they need to transfer you. They might hesitate. All of that is fine. Just hold the silence.

If they say no, don't get flustered. Try this: "I'd really prefer not to transfer my balance elsewhere, but I've received other offers. If there's anything you can do to make this more competitive, I'd love to stay with you."

That one line—mentioning other offers—puts pressure on them. They know your debt could walk away and go to a competitor. And that makes them way more likely to play ball.

If they say no again, ask to speak with someone who has more flexibility. That might mean a supervisor or someone in the retention department. These are the people who can actually bend the rules. Repeat the same lines. Stay calm. Don't ramble.

The more you do this, the easier it gets. And the more likely you are to hear "yes." Even if the win is small—say, a 2% reduction in APR—that adds up. On a $5,000 balance, that could mean hundreds of dollars over the course of a year. That's not pocket change. That's momentum.

So keep this script handy. Use it once a year. Use it every six months. Use it whenever your situation changes. Your debt isn't static, and your terms shouldn't be either.

This is how you fight back—not with rage, not with panic, but with calm, confident, practiced words. You don't need to scream to get results. You just need to ask the right way.

And now, you know exactly how to do that.

What to Say When You're Behind on Payments

If you're already behind on payments, it can feel like the walls are closing in. You see the red letters, the late fees, the voicemails stacking up. The instinct is to hide. Ignore it. Pretend it'll go away. But let's be clear: silence makes it worse. Delay stacks the damage. The longer you avoid it, the fewer options you'll have.

And here's the truth nobody tells you—most creditors are way more flexible when you're honest and early than when you're panicked and silent.

So this section isn't about shame. It's about strategy. Because being behind doesn't mean you're out of the game. It means it's time to stop running and start negotiating. And you do that by calling them—not when everything is back on track, but now. That call might feel like swallowing glass, but the moment you dial, you're taking your power back. You're stepping out of avoidance and into control. And that changes everything.

Start with this mindset: your goal isn't to fix everything in one call. Your goal is to open the door. To show up. To be the kind of customer they can work with. Because once you've made contact, you've got leverage. You're not a ghost. You're a real person who's trying. And effort counts more than perfection in these conversations.

Let's say you're two payments behind on a credit card. Maybe you missed one paycheck. Maybe life blew up—medical bill, car repair, job loss. Doesn't matter. You're in the hole, and you need a ladder, not a lecture. When you call, don't start with a speech. Keep it simple. Say: "Hi, I know I'm behind on my payments. I want to fix that. I'm going through a financial hardship, and I'd like to know what options are available to help me catch up."

Nine times out of ten, they'll pause. You've just moved yourself out of the "ignore" file and into the "possible solution" file. They'll look at your account. Sometimes, without even asking, they'll say, "Let me check if we can offer you a payment plan." Other times, you have to dig a little. Ask directly: "Do you offer any hardship programs? Can the fees be waived? Can we spread my past-due balance over the next few months?"

If they say, "We don't have any options," don't accept that as gospel. That's often the first line defense. You counter with, "I understand. Can I speak with someone in the hardship or retention department?" That's where the real tools live. The rep you get at first might be reading from a script. The second person? That's the one who can help.

Now, let's say you don't have the full past-due amount. That's okay. Offer something. Even if it's fifty bucks. Even if it feels small. Say, "I can't pay the full balance today, but I can pay [amount] right now to show good faith. I want to stay in communication and keep working toward resolving this." That gesture can be the difference between them freezing your account or working with you.

And if they start using scare tactics—talking about collections, credit damage, legal action—don't panic. That's pressure. Flip it. Say, "I'd like to avoid that, too. Let's talk through what we can do before it gets to that point." You've reframed the conversation from threat to solution.

Here's another trick: if you're dealing with a bank or lender that's being stubborn, call them at different times. Call on different days. Try again. You'll get different reps with different training, different moods, and sometimes, better solutions. Persistence is part of the plan.

And don't underestimate the emotional power of honesty. One reader emailed us after using this script with a medical bill that had gone unpaid for six months. She called, said exactly this: "I'm overwhelmed and behind, but I want to fix it. I can't pay it all today. Can we work something out?" They gave her a zero-interest plan over 12 months and dropped $100 in late fees. Just like that. Not because she knew finance—because she showed up.

Also, document everything. Date, time, who you talked to, what they said. Write it down. If they offer you a plan or waive a fee, ask for it in writing. Protect yourself. This isn't about trust—it's about tracking. You're building a paper trail that proves you're serious.

When you make that call, you take back control. You're not waiting for the hammer to drop. You're holding the hammer and asking how to build a solution.

Settling Debts in Collections (Without Getting Screwed)

Getting a call from a debt collector feels like being hunted. They're aggressive. They're trained to make you feel like you've failed. They'll say things like "final notice" or "legal action" or "you must respond today." But here's the truth they hope you don't know—you've still got rights. And you've still got power.

First thing you do is breathe. Debt in collections sounds scarier than it is. What's happened is this: the original creditor gave up on getting paid and sold your debt to a collection agency for pennies on the dollar. Now the agency is trying to collect the full amount from you to make a profit.

But here's your edge: they're already ahead financially. Which means they're often willing to settle for less. You don't owe the original amount anymore. You owe what you negotiate.

Step one is validation. Before you say a single word about paying, send them a debt validation letter. This is a formal request for proof. You want them to verify the amount, show they own the debt, and confirm that you actually owe it. Until they respond, they can't legally keep bugging you. This filters out fake collectors and resets the power dynamic.

Once the debt is validated, you go in with a plan. Never agree to the full amount right away. They bought that debt for 10–20 cents on the dollar. If they say you owe $2,000, offer $500. Say: "I'd like to resolve this. I can pay $500 as a lump sum to settle this account in full."

They'll usually counter higher. Maybe $800. Maybe $1,000. That's your window. Find the middle ground. You're not bargaining at a flea market—you're negotiating like a person who knows how this works. Don't offer more than you can actually pay. And don't let them pressure you to give banking info. Never do auto-pay. Use money orders, prepaid debit, or anything you control.

And this is critical: get it in writing. If they agree to settle, say: "Please send me a written agreement that states this debt will be marked as 'settled in full' or 'paid in full' with a $0 balance before I send payment." If they won't send that? Don't pay. You need the paper trail.

Some collectors will try scare tactics. "We're filing a judgment." "This could affect your taxes." Most of it is noise. Ask for proof. Stay calm. You can even say, "I know my rights under the Fair Debt Collection Practices Act. I want everything in writing." That usually shuts the nonsense down.

And don't forget to check your credit report afterward. Make sure the debt is marked correctly. If they reported anything shady, dispute it. You've got a legal right to accuracy.

Settling collections isn't about being desperate. It's about closing a door that doesn't serve you anymore. You're not just paying a bill. You're ending a chapter. You're saying: this no longer owns me. I'm done with it.

You're not weak for settling. You're smart. You're strategic. You're done letting this debt hang over you. That's how you walk out of collections with your head up—and your future intact.

How to Handle Aggressive Collectors (and Protect Your Sanity)

There's a special kind of stress that hits when your phone lights up and you see "unknown number." Deep down, you already know who it is. Another collector. Another voicemail that sounds like a threat. Another reminder that your debt isn't just numbers—it's someone chasing you, squeezing your anxiety like a vice. If that's your current reality, let's flip the script right now. Because you're not powerless here. You've got rights, you've got options, and most of all, you've got nothing to be ashamed of.

Aggressive debt collectors make money by making you panic. That's their whole strategy. They speak fast. They use legal-sounding phrases. They tell you you're running out of time. They want you scared so you'll act without thinking. But here's the truth—they're limited in what they can actually do. And once you know the rules, you can take control of the conversation instead of letting them run it.

Step one: understand your rights under the Fair Debt Collection Practices Act (FDCPA). Collectors cannot call you before 8 a.m. or after 9 p.m. They can't call you at work if you tell them not to. They can't threaten you with jail. They can't harass or intimidate you. And once you tell them—in writing—to stop calling, they have to. That's federal law. And if they break it, you can sue.

So here's what to do when one of these aggressive calls comes in. First, stay calm. That's your power. No matter how intense they sound, don't match their energy. You're not here to argue. You're here to document. Get their name, the company name, the debt they're calling about, and the amount. Then tell them: "I'm requesting that all future communication be in writing only. Do not contact me by phone." Follow up with a written letter saying the same thing. Certified mail. Return receipt. Keep a copy.

Now they have to back off. They can't call again. If they do, you've got proof, and you can report them to the Consumer Financial Protection Bureau or your state attorney general. You can even take them to court and win damages. You're not helpless. You're protected. You just need to use the tools you've got.

If they send letters, review them carefully. Make sure the debt is real. If anything looks off—wrong amount, debt you don't recognize, weird agency—you send a debt validation request. This forces them to prove they're legit. Many can't. Many give up when they see you're informed. You're not an easy target anymore.

If the debt is real and within the statute of limitations (usually 3–6 years depending on your state), you can choose to settle. But only on your terms. Never agree to anything on the phone. Never give banking info. Get every promise in writing first. And never, ever let them rush you. If they say you have to decide today, that's a lie. Take your time. Get clear. Then move forward with a plan.

Some of these collectors will try to break you down emotionally. They'll shame you. Mock you. Push your buttons. That's not business—it's bullying. And you don't have to take it. Hang up. Block the number. Report them. You don't owe anyone the right to ruin your day.

Here's a line you can use the next time they get loud: "I'm not refusing to pay. I'm asking for proper documentation, and I expect professional communication. If you can't provide that, this conversation is over." Then end the call. You don't need to argue. You don't need to explain your life story. You set boundaries and walk away.

And remember this—being in debt doesn't make you a bad person. It doesn't give anyone the right to harass you. You're dealing with a tough situation the best way you can. That's strength. That's courage. And with the right moves, this chapter will end. The stress will lift. The calls will stop. The balance will shrink.

You're not just surviving aggressive collectors. You're dismantling their power. One boundary at a time. One letter at a time. One win at a time.

This is how you protect your sanity, reclaim your voice, and remind the world that you're not to be pushed around. You've got this. And the collectors? They're about to find out they messed with the wrong one.

Emergency Funds That Actually Work (Even While You're Broke)

Let's start with a myth that needs to die: you're either paying off debt or building an emergency fund—but not both. That's nonsense. Yes, debt payoff is the priority. But if you've got zero dollars stashed for emergencies, you're basically building a house with no roof during hurricane season. One unexpected vet bill, car repair, or surprise layoff—and boom, your whole payoff plan explodes. That's not strategy. That's gambling.

Emergency funds aren't just a cushion. They're a weapon. They protect your momentum. They let you handle life without hitting pause on your progress. And the truth is, you don't need to wait until you're out of debt to start one. You need to build it while you're paying down what you owe. Because when the crap hits the fan—and it always does—it's that little stash that keeps you from reaching for the credit card again.

But let's be real: when you're living paycheck to paycheck, saving anything can feel like climbing Everest in flip-flops. You're not alone. The trick is not to aim for some magical "3–6 months of expenses" right out of the gate. That number is for later. The goal right now? Your first $500. That's it. That's the fund that changes everything.

Five hundred bucks won't fix every problem, but it'll soften the blow. It'll cover a busted tire, a broken phone, an unexpected fee, or a utility bill that suddenly doubled. More importantly, it gives you breathing room—the kind that stops panic spending before it starts.

So how do you build an emergency fund when every dollar already feels claimed? You get scrappy. You go on a temporary offensive. You flip couch cushions, you sell something, you babysit, you cut a few wants, you do a weird gig for one weekend. You make your own "crisis fund challenge." And you tell yourself: this isn't forever. It's just to hit that first $500. After that, we adjust.

One reader sent in this story: she delivered groceries on weekends for one month. Made $475, put it straight into a savings account labeled "Do Not Touch." The next month, her brakes failed. That $475 became the reason she didn't go further into debt. That's the power of being proactive. It's not sexy, but it works.

And yes—your emergency fund needs its own account. Don't keep it in your checking. That's not savings. That's just delayed spending. Set up a free online savings account, even if it earns you only pennies in interest. The point isn't growth. It's separation. It's psychological distance. When your emergency fund lives on its own island, you treat it differently. It becomes sacred.

Here's the rule: you only touch it when it's a real emergency. Not a "sale you can't miss." Not dinner because you forgot to meal prep. Not a birthday gift. We're talking car repair, medical expense, job loss, life-disrupting stuff. And if you use it? No guilt. That's what it's for. Just refill it before you throw more at your debt. Emergency fund gets priority status until it's back at full strength.

You're not weak for needing a safety net. You're smart for building one. Because the truth is, the world doesn't care if you're on a debt-free mission. Your water heater can still break. Your kid can still get sick. Your hours at work can still get cut. And when that happens, it's the people who planned ahead—just a little—who stay in control.

So don't let anyone shame you for pausing your debt snowball to stash some cash. That move doesn't mean you've lost momentum. It means you're protecting it. And that's what a real plan looks like.

The emergency fund isn't a luxury. It's a lifeline. You build it first, small and strong, then you go back to crushing debt like a machine. And when life hits? You hit back—with a plan, not a panic attack.

That's the move. That's the mindset. And that's how you win this game for good.

Why You Need Cash, Not Credit, When Life Blows Up

When disaster strikes, your instinct might be to reach for your credit card. After all, it's there, right? You swipe, solve the problem, and promise to figure it out later. But here's the catch: that "later" adds interest. That "later" becomes a bigger problem. That "later" traps you in the exact cycle you're trying to escape.

This is why cash—actual money you've saved—is so powerful. When you cover an emergency with your own cash, the crisis ends the moment you handle it. No interest. No balance haunting you. No mental load of yet another payment hanging over your head. It's done. It's clean. And that's a freedom credit can never give you.

Credit isn't a safety net. It's a loan wrapped in convenience. The moment you use it, you're borrowing against your future self. That might be okay in a real, true emergency. But the less you rely on credit, the faster you win the game. The more you flex your emergency fund, the more you break free from the trap that built the debt in the first place.

Let's paint two scenarios. Same emergency—a $700 car repair. In one version, you put it on a credit card. You're stressed, but relieved it's handled. Then the bill comes. You can't pay it all, so you pay the minimum. Over the next six months, you end up paying $900 for a $700 fix. You're still not caught up.

In the second version, you have a $500 emergency fund and $200 in your checking. You drain the emergency stash and add the rest. It hurts, but it's paid. You go to bed knowing you don't owe anyone. You're not behind. You're just ready to refill.

That's the real difference. Emergencies paid in cash end the moment the bill is covered. Emergencies paid on credit drag on. They grow. They multiply. And they mess with your momentum.

Some people argue, "I'd rather use the bank's money and keep mine." That's a mindset built for people who can afford risk. But if you're climbing out of debt, that's not your game right now. You're not playing with house money. You're rebuilding your own. And every time you choose cash over credit, you get stronger.

There's also the mental weight of using credit for crises. It doesn't feel like a solution—it feels like a bandage on a bullet wound. You handled the moment, sure, but you didn't solve the pattern. The next time something breaks, you'll panic again. You'll swipe again. And you'll feel even more stuck.

Cash, on the other hand, creates peace. Even if it's just a few hundred dollars. Even if it's not perfect. Knowing you have something set aside changes how you walk through life. It quiets the stress. It gives you room to think clearly instead of react wildly. It creates space between you and chaos.

So let's stop treating credit as a fallback plan. It's not. It's a delay tactic dressed up like a solution. You want real power? Build your emergency stash. Use it when life punches you in the gut. Then refill it like your freedom depends on it—because it does.

That's how you stop emergencies from becoming debt triggers. That's how you break the panic loop. That's how you take control—for real.

The $500 Buffer Plan: Build It Fast, Guard It Hard

The first $500 you save is the most important money you'll ever have. Not because it's a fortune—but because it's your first real defense. It turns chaos into inconvenience. It buys you space. It proves to yourself that you can save money, even when everything feels tight.

This isn't about long-term savings. This is your "oh crap" fund. A blown tire, a sudden copay, a forgotten bill. Life doesn't pause while you pay off debt, and this $500 buffer is how you stay in the game when things get messy.

Here's the plan: build it fast. Don't wait for extra money. Go create it. Look at your next 30 days like a challenge. What can you cut? What can you flip? What can you hustle? This is short-term intensity, not forever. Sell stuff. Skip takeout. Deliver food. Babysit. Pick up one weekend gig. Turn your clutter into cash and your time into buffer money.

One guy we talked to made his $500 in two weeks by walking dogs on his lunch break and selling two old phones. Another turned her closet clean-out into $350 on Facebook Marketplace. It doesn't have to be big. It just has to be fast.

Because the faster you build the buffer, the faster you break the habit of using credit as a crutch.

Once you hit $500, guard it like it's sacred. This isn't fun money. This isn't upgrade-your-iPhone money. This is only-for-bad-days money. The kind that saves your ass when the world decides to test you.

Keep it separate. Put it in a savings account with a name like "Emergency Only" or "Break Glass Here." You want visual and mental separation from your spending money. That tiny bit of friction—the fact that it's not in your checking account—makes it harder to dip into.

And here's the mindset shift: if you have to use it, that's not failure. That's the plan working. The emergency came. You handled it. You didn't panic. You didn't swipe. You didn't fall back into debt. You bought yourself peace.

After you use it? Pause your debt snowball. Refill the buffer. Always refill first. It's your armor. You don't go into battle with your chest wide open.

This $500 won't fix everything, but it changes everything. It's your proof that progress is possible. That you're not powerless. That even broke, overwhelmed, or starting from zero—you can build something that protects you.

And once that belief sets in? The rest gets easier. Because the hardest part of money isn't math. It's momentum. And this little buffer is where that starts.

Build it fast. Guard it hard. And let it be the first win of many.

Where to Stash It: High-Yield Accounts and Safe Spots

Once you've scraped together your emergency buffer, the next question is: where do you put it? Not emotionally—we already covered that—but physically. Where does this money live so it's safe, protected, and doesn't accidentally get absorbed into your everyday spending?

Short answer: not in your checking account. Your checking account is where money goes to disappear. Bills, subscriptions, food delivery, gas, random late-night online impulse purchases—checking accounts are a war zone for your dollars. You don't want your emergency fund hanging out there, watching your bank balance drop every day like a horror movie.

Your emergency fund deserves its own space. Preferably in a high-yield savings account (HYSA). Why? Because it earns you a little something for doing absolutely nothing. Is it going to make you rich? No. But even 4% interest is way better than letting your money sit in a traditional savings account earning 0.01%, which is basically nothing. At 4%, $500 becomes $520+ over a year—and that's without lifting a finger.

But it's not just about interest. It's about friction. You want your emergency money to be easy to get if you need it, but not so easy that you spend it on pizza or panic buys. That's why an online savings account works so well. There's a built-in 1–2 day transfer delay to move money back into checking, which is just enough time to ask, "Is this really an emergency, or am I just bored?"

Some of the best HYSAs are with online banks like Ally, Capital One 360, SoFi, Discover, or Marcus. They don't charge monthly fees, and they let you nickname your savings account. Name it something that'll make you pause before touching it. "Emergency Only" is fine. But if you're spicy, try "Touch This and Regret It" or "Future Me's Lifeline." Give it a personality. Make it memorable.

Now, if you're old-school or hate online banking, you've still got options. You can open a traditional savings account at a credit union and keep your debit card in a drawer. Just make sure it's not connected to your checking account with auto-transfers, or that "buffer" will get drained faster than you can say overdraft.

What about cash? Is it smart to keep some emergency money in literal bills? Sometimes, yes. Cash still works in power outages. If your card gets frozen or there's fraud, having $100 or $200 stashed at home can make a big difference. But don't go full doomsday prepper and bury jars in the backyard. Keep it in a safe, out of sight, where kids, roommates, or nosy friends can't stumble across it.

Also: don't forget about psychological safety. When you separate your emergency fund from your day-to-day money, you reduce decision fatigue. You stop having to ask, "Can I afford this?" every five minutes. The line is already drawn. Your emergency fund isn't part of the debate. It's there for when life explodes, not when you're craving sushi.

Having the right place to stash your fund isn't just about dollars. It's about clarity. It's about making it harder to screw yourself over. It's about making smart the default and dumb the exception.

That's the strategy. Create separation. Add friction. Make access possible but not instant. And give that little pile of protection the home it deserves.

When to Pause Your Debt Snowball to Refill Your Fund

You're crushing debt, paying off balances, throwing every spare dollar at your credit cards like a boss—and then life decides to slap you across the face. Your car breaks down. Your dog needs emergency surgery. You drop your phone in a toilet and it's not coming back. Suddenly, you need $400 and the only thing standing between you and another round of credit card debt is your emergency fund.

So you use it. You drain it. You handle the problem. Crisis averted. But now what? Do you go right back to hammering your debt with every penny? Nope. You hit pause.

This part is hard for a lot of people, especially the go-getters. The ones who feel like any month they're not knocking out balances is a month wasted. But refilling your emergency fund is not lost progress—it's protecting your progress. Because the next emergency is always coming. And if you've got nothing saved when it hits, guess what? You're right back where you started.

Here's the rule: after you use your emergency fund, you pause your debt snowball. Not forever. Just long enough to get your buffer back up. Whether that's $500 or $1,000 or whatever your number is, that comes first. That's your new target. It becomes your minimum safety net before you throw another dollar at debt.

Think of your emergency fund like armor. You don't head back into battle with holes in your gear. You patch the damage, then go swing the sword. Otherwise, one hit and you're down again.

Let's walk through it. Say you used $350 from your emergency fund to fix your car. You've been throwing $400 a month at debt. Instead, this month, that $400 goes straight into the emergency fund. You're not losing steam. You're rebuilding your shield. That move means the next time life punches you, you don't flinch—you're covered.

And no, you don't need to stop every single extra debt payment forever. If you want to do a 50/50 split—half to the fund, half to debt—you can. But don't pretend the emergency fund is optional. It's not. It's survival money. And treating it like a luxury will only keep you stuck.

A reader once told us she felt like she was "cheating on her debt plan" when she paused payments to refill her buffer. That mindset is poison. Your debt doesn't care how fast you pay it off. But your mental health? Your stress levels? Your peace of mind? They care deeply. And nothing feeds burnout faster than feeling like you can't breathe because every dollar is already spoken for.

So refill the fund. Do it fast. Sell something. Pick up a gig. Redirect bonuses. Whatever it takes. You don't need perfection—you need protection. Once you've hit your buffer goal again, get right back to crushing that debt.

That's the rhythm. Push hard. Protect yourself. Push again.

It's not a detour. It's the strategy. Because this isn't just about paying things off—it's about staying free once you are.

And that's the whole point.

How to Grow It Without Slowing Down Your Progress

Once you've built your initial buffer—your $500 or your $1,000—there comes a point when you start asking, should I grow this thing? Should I build a full-blown emergency fund? And if I do, won't that slow down my debt payoff?

The answer is yes—and no. It depends on how you do it. Because here's the trick: you don't have to throw your whole engine into savings. You don't need to stop your momentum. You just need to keep adding drops of fuel to that emergency tank while your main fire burns hot on the debt.

Here's the mindset: your emergency fund isn't a destination. It's a habit. Something you build alongside everything else. Because once your basic buffer is set, growing it doesn't have to be your main financial goal—it just has to stay alive. That means adding small, regular deposits. It means throwing extra money at it when the opportunity shows up. It means planting seeds, not building barns.

A great way to grow your fund without killing your payoff progress is to redirect small windfalls. Tax refund? Send 80% to debt, 20% to savings. Birthday money? Refund check? Tiny side gig payment? Let a slice of that drip into your emergency stash. You don't need to put hundreds away each month. You just need to be consistent. Over time, those slices add up.

Let's say you add just $25 a week to your fund after hitting your initial $500. That's $100 a month. At the end of a year, you've got $1,700 saved. That's how you turn a small start into real security—without ever taking your foot off the gas.

Another trick? Automate it. Set up an automatic transfer for whatever feels manageable—$10, $25, $50—from checking to savings each payday. You'll barely feel it, and it builds quietly in the background. This isn't about being aggressive. It's about being intentional. You're not saving to feel good. You're saving to stay ready.

And here's the other part people don't talk about: your emergency fund doesn't have to live on an island. It can evolve. Let's say you hit $1,000 and feel good. Then your car gets older, your health changes, your job gets less stable. Suddenly, that $1,000 doesn't feel like enough. That's okay. Your emergency fund should match your life stage. If you've got kids, pets, a home—your number will be different than someone living solo in a studio apartment. So reassess as you grow.

But no matter where you are, don't let the goal of a bigger emergency fund paralyze your debt payoff. Think of it like a garden hose filling two buckets. Most of the flow goes to debt. But you let a slow, steady drip keep the emergency fund alive. That way, when life throws a punch, you've still got cushion. You don't panic. You don't pause. You just pivot for a moment and keep going.

And if you ever hit a point where your fund feels "full"—great. Let it sit. Keep it ready. Don't touch it unless life really swings hard. And if you do have to use it, you already know the drill: pause the snowball, refill, restart. No guilt. No panic. Just process.

Remember, the goal isn't to hoard money. The goal is to protect your momentum. To avoid sabotage. To stay in control even when life gets messy.

So yes, grow your emergency fund. But don't wait until it's "done" to tackle your debt. You can build both. You can flex both. You can be prepared and still aggressive. That's the balance.

And once you master it, you stop living in fear. Because now, you're not hoping nothing bad happens—you're ready for it. That's real power. That's real peace. And that's exactly how you win for good.

Debt and Your Brain — Outsmarting the Traps That Keep You Stuck

If getting out of debt was purely about math, you'd already be done. Add the income, subtract the expenses, cut the lattes, rinse, repeat. But we both know it's not just math. It's psychology. It's emotion. It's habits, fears, impulses, and invisible mental traps that screw up your plan even when the numbers make sense.

Debt messes with your head. It fogs your thinking. It makes you feel small, guilty, behind. You start making decisions from a place of stress instead of strategy. You avoid looking at your balances. You tell yourself, "I'll deal with it later." And that's how the cycle continues—not because you're lazy, but because your brain is wired to avoid pain.

Understanding how your brain reacts to debt is the key to breaking that cycle. Because once you see the traps, you can dodge them. Once you know the mental games, you can start playing your own.

One of the biggest traps is debt fatigue. That moment when you've been grinding for months, maybe years, and you start thinking, "What's the point?" You're tired. You want a break. You want a taste of freedom. So you splurge. You take your foot off the gas. And boom—you lose momentum, rack up more interest, and feel like you're back at square one.

This isn't a discipline problem. It's a brain chemistry problem. Your brain gets addicted to novelty and dopamine. And debt payoff? It's the long game. It's delayed gratification. So if you're not building in small wins—weekly victories, progress checkmarks, visual trackers—you'll burn out.

Another trap? All-or-nothing thinking. You miss a payment, and suddenly your brain screams, "You blew it!" So you stop trying altogether. One mistake turns into a spiral. But the truth is, one off month doesn't erase your progress. One wrong step doesn't kick you back to the start. The win is in showing up again the next day, even after you fall.

There's also the shame spiral. That nasty voice in your head that says you're bad with money, that you deserve this mess, that you'll never dig out. Shame is the glue that keeps people stuck. It disconnects you from logic and locks you into self-sabotage. The antidote to shame is curiosity. Instead of asking, "What's wrong with me?" start asking, "What's actually going on here?" Be the investigator, not the judge.

Then there's comparison. You see someone on Instagram paying off $40K in 10 months and think, "Why am I not doing that?" You feel like you're losing, even if you're making progress. But their race isn't yours. You don't know their income, their help, their privileges. You're not behind—you're on your path. And comparing only steals energy you need to keep going.

Last but not least, beware of the normalcy bias. That's the voice that says, "Everyone has debt. It's just the way life works." No. It's not. Debt might be common, but it's not required. You don't have to live this way forever. That belief alone—"I can change this"—is the first crack in the wall.

Your brain isn't broken. It's just trying to protect you. But it's using the wrong tools. So give it new ones. Build habits. Create triggers that remind you why you're doing this. Write your goals on your bathroom mirror. Use sticky notes. Set calendar reminders. Track your wins. Reward yourself without spending. Make your environment work for you, not against you.

Outsmarting debt isn't just about throwing money at it—it's about staying in the game long enough to win. And that means treating your brain like a partner, not a saboteur. Understand it. Train it. Work with it. And when it slips? Forgive, reset, and keep going.

Because the truth is, you don't just need a better budget—you need a better mindset. One that says, "I know this is hard. I know I'm human. But I'm doing it anyway."

That's how people win. Not with perfection. With persistence. With grit. With a brain that learns, adjusts, and keeps swinging.

This is where everything shifts. Where you stop seeing debt as a math problem and start seeing it for what it really is—a brain game you're built to win.

The Psychology of Spending — Why Your Brain Loves the Swipe

Your brain is not your enemy—but it sure doesn't always make it easy to stay out of debt. If you've ever stood in a store and thought, "I shouldn't buy this," and then five seconds later swiped your card anyway, congratulations: you've experienced the full force of your brain's reward system hijacking your logic. That tug, that moment of impulse, is powered by dopamine—the brain's favorite little hit of joy.

Dopamine is released when your brain anticipates a reward, not even when you get it. That's why just scrolling Amazon or adding things to a cart can feel good. It's not about the item. It's about the feeling. The rush. The illusion of control or comfort or success. When you swipe that card, your brain lights up like you just did something amazing—even if the aftermath is financial regret and interest charges.

Marketers know this. Stores are designed to trigger spending. Sale signs in red. Smells that remind you of childhood. Items placed strategically near checkout. All of it is meant to bypass your thinking brain and hit your emotional brain—the one that says, "Treat yourself," even when your checking account is already holding on by a thread.

Credit cards make it even easier. They separate the pain of paying from the act of buying. When you spend cash, your brain registers a small loss—it feels real. But when you swipe, it's disconnected. It doesn't feel like you're losing anything. That's why people spend more with credit than cash, even when they have the cash in hand.

Understanding this isn't about guilt. It's about defense. If you know your brain is chasing dopamine, you can start feeding it differently. You don't need to eliminate pleasure—you need to redirect it. What else can trigger that same hit? Crossing something off a checklist. Moving a paperclip on a debt tracker. Watching your savings go up, even a few bucks. Those moments are dopamine, too.

Another way to outsmart the impulse loop is to build a pause into your purchases. Create friction. Unlink your cards from online stores. Add a 24-hour rule to any non-essential buy. Put a sticky note on your debit card that says, "Do I want this or need this?" Small barriers short-circuit the autopilot mode your brain loves so much.

And if you do make an impulse purchase? Don't spiral. Don't burn the whole plan down. Get curious. What were you feeling before that buy? Stressed? Bored? Lonely? Your spending is usually a symptom. Find the feeling underneath, and you can start solving the real problem.

The goal isn't to become a robot who never enjoys life. It's to stop letting your brain's craving for quick rewards sabotage your long-term peace. It's to retrain your brain to see progress as the new pleasure. That's how you shift from short-term dopamine to long-term freedom.

You don't need more willpower. You need better tools. Better inputs. Better scripts. Because once you understand how your brain works, you stop blaming yourself—and you start building systems that work with your wiring instead of against it.

Motivation Is a Muscle — How to Stay Fired Up Without Burning Out

You start strong. Fired up. Motivated. Ready to destroy your debt. You build a spreadsheet. You post your goal. You make your first few payments and feel like a legend. And then—life happens. Something breaks. Your energy dips. You have a bad day. Suddenly, the momentum slows. You miss a step. And that high? Gone.

This is the point where most people give up. Not because they don't want it anymore—but because they thought motivation would carry them the whole way. It won't. Motivation is not a fuel tank. It's a match. It lights the fire, but it doesn't keep it burning. You need structure. You need systems. You need grit.

And you need to treat motivation like a muscle—something you can train, flex, and rebuild when it gets weak.

One of the best ways to keep motivation alive is to measure progress visually. Human brains are wired to crave completion. That's why crossing off a to-do list feels so good. Use that. Make a chart. A tracker. A thermometer. A wall of sticky notes with each one representing $100 paid off. Every time you knock one out, remove a note. Watch the wall shrink. Watch your brain eat it up.

You also need to celebrate small wins. Don't wait until you're debt-free to feel good. Celebrate every milestone—first $100, first credit card closed, first month under budget. Create rewards that don't wreck your budget. Cheap treats, a night off, a dance party in your kitchen. Whatever makes it real.

Another trick? Revisit your why. When the grind gets boring, when the numbers feel slow, pull out the list. Why are you doing this? What will change when you're debt-free? Write it down again. Make it emotional. Make it vivid. Tape it to your fridge. You don't just want less debt—you want freedom, sleep, peace, security. That's what keeps you moving.

And sometimes, the best thing you can do is rest. Not quit. Just pause. Take a weekend off from thinking about money. Go for a walk. Watch a movie. Stop tracking for a day. Burnout isn't proof that you're failing—it's proof that you've been trying hard. Let your brain reset. Then come back with fresh eyes.

Staying fired up doesn't mean staying intense every second. It means staying in the game. Knowing your energy will rise and fall, and committing to show up anyway. Some days will be fire. Some days will be a flicker. Either way, you keep the spark alive.

Motivation isn't magic. It's built. And you're already building it, every time you choose progress over perfection.

This is the muscle. And you're stronger than you think.

Habit Hacking — Build Systems That Work When You Don't Feel Like It

Let's be honest. You won't always feel like doing the right thing. You won't always feel like making the payment, skipping the takeout, logging the expense. And that's fine—because willpower is not the goal. The goal is to build systems that work even when you don't. That's how real change sticks.

Habits are just decisions you've put on autopilot. They're shortcuts your brain creates to save energy. The trick is to make your good choices so easy, so automatic, that you barely have to think about them. That means setting up routines, triggers, and defaults that do the heavy lifting for you.

For example, you don't need to "feel motivated" to save money if you've already set up an automatic transfer to your emergency fund every payday. It just happens. You don't need to "remember" to check your spending if you've built a 5-minute money review into your Sunday morning coffee ritual. It becomes part of your week. Normal. Automatic. That's the win.

Start with anchor habits. These are actions you already do every day—brushing your teeth, making coffee, locking the door at night. Attach a new habit to one of those. Every morning after you brush your teeth, glance at your bank account. Every time you put gas in your car, write down how much you spent. Make it small. Make it consistent. Consistency beats intensity.

You also want to remove friction. If checking your budget feels like a chore, it's probably because the tool is too complicated. Simplify it. Use a notebook. Use an app you actually like. Don't aim for the perfect system—aim for the one you'll use. The habit that happens is better than the perfect plan that gathers dust.

One reader shared that she kept forgetting to log her spending, so she made it a rule: "Every night before I plug in my phone to charge, I update my tracker." After two weeks, it felt weird not to do it. That's how you know it's working. It didn't rely on her being in the mood. It relied on her environment doing the remembering.

Another trick is habit bundling. If you already watch Netflix every evening, pair it with a five-minute budget check. If you brew coffee each morning, use that time to look at yesterday's expenses. The goal is to make your money habits as natural and routine as brushing your teeth or scrolling your phone.

Visual cues work wonders, too. Put a sticky note on your mirror with your savings goal. Set your phone background to a photo of what being debt-free looks like for you—maybe it's peace, maybe it's travel, maybe it's just fewer panic attacks. Put reminders where your impulses usually win. If Amazon gets you at night, put a sticky note on your laptop: "Will this purchase matter in 48 hours?" That one question has saved people hundreds.

And build in checkpoints. Once a week, sit down and track your progress. Don't just rely on memory—see the numbers. See the changes. See the proof that you're moving forward. That kind of feedback is powerful. It fuels the next step, the next habit, the next win.

Habits aren't built in a day, but every time you follow through—even once—you're casting a vote for the kind of person you want to become. Each vote strengthens the identity. And when the identity is strong enough, the behavior follows automatically.

So don't chase discipline. Build structure. Build defaults. Build habits that are stronger than your mood. That's how people escape debt, stay out, and never look back.

Emotional Spending — What You're Really Buying (and How to Stop)

Emotional spending doesn't look like a meltdown. It looks like boredom scrolling, retail therapy, or rewarding yourself after a rough week. It's that subtle shift from "I want this" to "I need this to feel better." And it's sneaky. Because often, you don't even realize you're doing it.

Here's the truth: when you spend emotionally, you're not buying the thing—you're buying the feeling you hope the thing will give you. Comfort. Control. Escape. Identity. Sometimes it works—for a second. But then the dopamine fades, and all you're left with is more stuff and less money.

We're emotional creatures. Spending isn't just a transaction. It's often a response to something deeper: loneliness, stress, frustration, insecurity. And until you name that feeling, it will keep driving your behavior from the backseat. The spending becomes a way of self-soothing, like a sugar hit for the soul. Except it costs interest.

So how do you stop?

Start by noticing the pattern. Are there certain times of day you're more likely to shop online? Are there specific emotions that lead to swiping your card? Do certain people or situations trigger it? Track it. Name it. Write it down. "I shopped after that fight." "I scrolled Amazon when I felt ignored." Patterns create power—because once you see them, you can interrupt them.

Next, build a pause into your process. You don't have to ban shopping altogether—you just need to create space between the urge and the action. Try a 24-hour rule. Try writing the item on a list and waiting three days. Most of the time, the urge passes. And if it doesn't, you've had time to decide if it's actually worth it.

Then: replace the behavior. If shopping gives you comfort, what else could? A phone call. A walk. A journal entry. A workout. A funny video. Something that soothes without sabotaging. You're not trying to remove joy—you're just trying to stop the damage. Emotional spending is not about the item. It's about regulation. So give yourself other ways to regulate.

One woman we talked to kept a "Buy Later" list on her phone. Anytime she wanted something, she added it there instead of buying. She reviewed it once a month. Most items didn't even make sense anymore. But the list helped her feel in control. She wasn't saying "no"—she was saying "not yet." That small shift saved her hundreds.

Another strategy is to budget for emotional spending—on purpose. Give yourself a small "fun fund." Maybe it's $20 a month. You still get to treat yourself, but you're doing it on your terms, with boundaries. It's not a runaway reaction—it's a conscious choice.

And when you mess up? Don't spiral. Curiosity beats shame every time. Ask, "What was I really feeling?" Then try again. Progress over perfection.

Emotional spending loses its grip when you stop hiding from the emotion. When you face it, name it, and meet it with something better. And the better you get at that, the less power money has over your feelings.

Debt freedom isn't just a numbers game. It's an emotional game. You win by knowing yourself, protecting your peace, and creating habits that support—not sabotage—your healing.

And the more you do that, the less you'll need a shopping cart to feel whole.

Rewrite Your Money Story — Identity, Shame, and the New You

Most people carry a money story they never chose. It came from childhood, from family, from culture. Maybe it sounded like "we don't talk about money," or "money is always tight," or "people like us just don't get ahead." You didn't write it, but it's been playing in the background for years, shaping your habits, your fears, and your financial decisions.

To crush your debt and stay free, you need more than strategies and spreadsheets. You need a new story. One that's written by you, for you, about who you are now—not who you used to be. This is the identity shift. The part where you stop seeing yourself as someone who's "bad with money" and start seeing yourself as someone who's learning, growing, and getting strong.

Shame is one of the biggest blocks to this shift. It tells you that your past mistakes define you. That if you were smarter, more disciplined, more responsible, you wouldn't be in this mess. Shame doesn't just say you did something wrong. It says you are something wrong. And that's a lie.

Shame thrives in silence. It gets louder when you avoid the truth. The cure isn't pretending the past didn't happen—it's dragging it into the light and saying, "Yes, that was me. But it's not who I am now." When you tell your story honestly, you rob shame of its power. You take the wheel back.

Let's say you've got $20K in credit card debt. You might think that makes you irresponsible. But look closer. Maybe that debt came from surviving—medical bills, job loss, helping family. Maybe it came from a lack of education—no one taught you how interest works, how budgets work, how compound debt traps people. That doesn't mean you're bad. It means you've been trying your best with limited tools. And now? You're getting new ones.

Changing your money identity starts with language. Stop saying "I'm just bad with money." That's not identity, that's programming. Start saying, "I'm learning how to handle money differently." Speak the future into the present. Say what you're becoming, not what you've been.

Build rituals around this new identity. Every time you make a payment, say it out loud: "This is me taking control." Every time you check your balance, even if it stings, say, "This is me facing truth with courage." It sounds small, even cheesy, but repetition rewires the brain. Affirmations don't make things true—they reinforce the truth you're choosing to believe.

You can also rewrite your story literally. Take five minutes and write down your old money story. What did you believe growing up? What patterns did you absorb? Then, flip the script. Write your new story. "I used to think debt was normal. Now I know freedom is possible." "I used to avoid money. Now I face it with clarity." This isn't fluff. It's mental muscle.

And while you're at it—find proof. Your brain loves evidence. So give it some. List five things you've done differently in the last month. Maybe you canceled a subscription. Maybe you made an extra payment. Maybe you read a book (like this one) instead of ignoring your finances. Those wins are bricks in your new foundation. Stack them.

You are not your balance. You are not your lowest financial moment. You are not your past paycheck or your current credit score. You are the person taking action now. You are the one interrupting cycles. You are writing a story that ends with freedom.

Debt doesn't get to be your label. It's just a chapter. And starting today, you get to decide how the next one goes. So choose bold. Choose clear. Choose proud. Not because it's easy—but because it's yours.

You don't owe the world an apology for waking up. You don't owe shame any more rent in your head. What you owe is a future version of yourself—the one who wakes up debt-free, calm, confident, and clear.

That version starts here. With this story. With this shift. With you.

The 12-Month Payoff Plan — Make It Real, Make It Yours

You've got the tools now. The psychology, the systems, the fire. You've learned how debt works, how your brain works, how life likes to throw curveballs and how you can catch them without falling back into old habits. This is where it all comes together. It's time to build your own 12-month payoff plan. Not a cookie-cutter fantasy. Not a rigid blueprint that only works if you're a robot with a perfect income and zero emergencies. This is real life. So the plan has to be real too.

Start with clarity. Open up every account you owe money on—every card, every loan, every debt that's been hanging over your head like a thundercloud. Write down the balance, the interest rate, the minimum payment. Stare it in the face. This is the part most people skip because it sucks. But you can't escape a maze you refuse to map.

Once you've got your list, you're going to choose your weapon: avalanche or snowball. Avalanche saves the most money long-term—target the highest interest rate first. Snowball builds motivation fastest—target the smallest balance and knock it out quick. Both work. Pick the one that fits your psychology, not someone else's spreadsheet. Are you motivated by saving dollars or stacking wins? There's no wrong answer, just your answer.

Then, it's time to do the math. How much can you actually throw at debt each month? Not your dream number. Your real number. After rent, food, transportation, and survival essentials, what's left? If it's $300, great. If it's $30, also great. This isn't about shame—it's about starting from truth.

With your total monthly number in hand, you assign the minimums to all debts except the one you're targeting first. That one gets all the extra. Every month. Relentlessly. No second guessing. You repeat that until it's gone, then roll that payment into the next one. That's the snowball. Or the avalanche. Either way, it's movement.

But here's the real magic: 12 months isn't just a timeframe—it's a mindset. It's a stake in the ground. You're declaring war on this debt. You're saying, "No matter how long it actually takes, I'm acting like this is my year." Because that energy shifts your decisions. It makes you hustle harder. It makes you get creative. It turns you into someone who's chasing freedom, not just waiting for it.

So you go all in. You trim fat from the budget. You cancel the stuff you forgot you were paying for. You sell something you haven't touched in a year. You take on one weird weekend side gig and throw all of it at your target debt. Every extra dollar becomes a brick in your exit path.

And here's what people miss: your 12-month payoff plan isn't rigid. It breathes. Life happens. You might have a setback. That's not failure—it's reality. When it happens, you don't scrap the plan. You adjust it. You refill the emergency fund, then get back on the path. This plan doesn't break under pressure. It bends with you.

And you track. Oh man, you track. Because progress without visibility is invisible. Create a visual. Fill in a bar. Move paper clips. Color in a thermometer. Watch it shrink. Celebrate the milestones. $1,000 paid off? That's huge. One card closed? That's freedom. Five months in and you haven't quit? That's a new identity.

By month twelve, maybe you're done. Maybe you're close. Maybe you've still got a little to go. Doesn't matter. You'll be a different person. You'll know how to manage your money, how to handle setbacks, how to keep showing up even when motivation fades. That's the real win.

This isn't the end of your story. It's the part where the fog clears and you finally see what's possible. Debt doesn't own you anymore. You've got a plan. You've got power. And you've got twelve months to prove it—to yourself, to your future, to everyone who told you it couldn't be done.

So draw the line. Make your chart. Pick your method. Build your system. This is your 12-month transformation. You don't need perfect conditions. You just need to begin.

Start where you are. Use what you have. Move every single week. And when you look up a year from now, you won't just be out of debt—you'll be unrecognizable.

In the best way possible.

That's the plan. Now go make it yours.

The First 30 Days — Momentum Over Perfection

The first month isn't about perfection. It's about movement. Day one, you're fired up. You've read the book. You've made your decision. But what you do next is what really matters. This isn't about waiting for everything to line up. It's about starting messy and building from there. In the first 30 days, your only job is to prove to yourself that you can move forward—even when it's uncomfortable.

Start by making your debt list and choosing your payoff strategy. Avalanche or snowball—pick it, commit to it, and stop second-guessing. The faster you make that decision, the faster you take action. Then, go get your baseline numbers. Income, bills, and real monthly spending. Don't guess—pull up your last two months of transactions and see where your money has been sneaking off to. Print out your statements and highlight every nonessential item. Add it up. That's not just spending—that's opportunity.

Now, it's time to get scrappy. Where can you find extra cash in the next four weeks? Not forever—just this month. Could you sell something you're not using? Could you cancel one streaming service or eat at home twice instead of going out? These aren't sacrifices—they're signals. They tell your brain, "We're serious now."

Once you've freed up that money, make your first big extra debt payment—even if it's just fifty bucks. The amount isn't what matters. The action is. You're flipping the script. You're taking control. That first payment sets the tone for everything else. Take a picture of your payment confirmation. Write "I did this" next to it. Save it. Frame it if you want. That's your Day One.

Expect resistance. You might feel like quitting after a week. Your budget might blow up. You might forget to track spending or hit a rough patch emotionally. That's normal. That's expected. The win is in sticking with it anyway. Progress happens when you keep moving through the mess, not when you avoid it. Write that down somewhere: Motion beats perfection.

The best way to keep momentum going is visibility. You need to see your wins as they happen. Create a debt tracker. Make it visual. Update it weekly. Seeing the numbers drop—even a little—will keep your brain engaged and motivated. You're literally reprogramming your reward system to crave progress.

Build in a quick weekly review. Fifteen minutes every Sunday night. Look at what went right, what didn't, and what you're adjusting. That little check-in is where consistency is born. That's where your progress locks in. Journal a few lines if you need to. Ask, "What helped me this week?" and "What tripped me up?" Now you're learning in real time.

Stack your tools early. Use a simple app or notebook for tracking. Set text reminders for due dates. Use browser extensions to block online shopping sites if that's a weakness. Treat your environment like your teammate. Set it up to catch you before you slip.

By the end of the first 30 days, you don't need to be perfect. You just need to be in motion. With a working budget, a selected strategy, a visual tracker, and at least one extra payment made, you're already further ahead than most people ever get. And more importantly, you've started rewiring how you deal with money.

This month isn't about solving the whole problem. It's about showing yourself you can. And that's how real transformation starts. The snowball isn't just about debt—it's about identity. Once you prove to yourself that you're someone who acts, the game changes.

Budget Like a Boss — Flexible Frameworks That Actually Work

Most people hate budgeting because they've been taught it's a punishment. A restrictive diet for your wallet. But a real budget isn't a set of rules—it's a mirror.

It shows you what you care about. It shows you what's working and what isn't. And when it's done right, it becomes one of the most freeing tools in your debt-killing arsenal.

Here's the deal: you don't need a spreadsheet with 73 categories and color-coded formulas. You need a budget that reflects your real life, not your fantasy version. You need something flexible, fast, and honest.

Start with your non-negotiables. What must get paid to keep life running? Rent, groceries, gas, utilities—your survival stack. Then figure out your real spending. Not your ideal spending, your actual spending. Most people underestimate their costs by hundreds because they round down or forget things like takeout, coffee, gifts, and random "emergencies." Pull your last two bank statements and face the truth.

Once you have your numbers, create a simple plan. Income minus fixed bills minus flexible spending equals what you can throw at debt. If that number is zero—or negative—don't panic. That's information. That tells you something needs to shift. And now you're finally looking at it with open eyes.

The magic is in iteration. Your first budget will suck. That's okay. Think of it as your "draft budget." Expect to adjust. Expect to miss something. Your budget is a living document. The goal isn't to nail it perfectly every month—the goal is to make it more accurate every month. It's not set in stone. It's set in motion.

Try the "80/20 budget" if you want simplicity. Use 80% of your income for living expenses and debt, and stash or save the other 20%. Or use the envelope method—digital or physical. Give every dollar a job. The method doesn't matter as much as your consistency with it. If you track it and tweak it, it'll work.

And don't forget to budget for fun. Even when you're in debt payoff mode. A strict budget with zero room for joy is a budget you'll abandon by week three. Give yourself a small "fun" category. It's not weakness—it's strategy. It keeps you sane.

Set up auto-drafts for essentials. Put your due dates in a calendar. Make your budget hard to forget. If it lives in a Google Sheet you open once a month, it's not a system—it's a suggestion. You want it baked into your routines. Budgeting should become as normal as checking your phone.

Most importantly, stop treating budgeting like a chore. Treat it like a tool that buys you clarity, freedom, and peace. The people who succeed aren't the ones with the most complex plans. They're the ones who keep showing up, month after month, tweaking the plan, fixing what's broken, and moving forward. Every time you look at your money, you're saying, "I'm not hiding anymore." That changes everything.

Your budget is your map. It won't always be perfect, but it'll keep you out of the woods. And that's what matters. No more guessing. No more avoiding. Just a clear plan you trust.

In the next section, we'll build the toolkit that makes this map easier to follow every step of the way.

The Toolkit — Apps, Systems, and Routines That Do the Work With You

You don't need to be a financial wizard to win at money—you just need the right tools doing the heavy lifting. Most people try to willpower their way through debt with nothing but vibes and frustration. That works for maybe a week. Then life happens, your brain gets tired, and the old patterns come storming back. The fix? Build a toolkit that makes the right thing the easy thing. The goal here is to automate, simplify, and repeat. You're not trying to think harder—you're trying to think less and win more.

Let's start with tracking tools. If you're a pen-and-paper person, get a notebook that lives in your bag or on your nightstand. Write your spending down once a day, even if it's just a sticky note. That act of writing builds awareness. And awareness is half the battle. If you're digital, grab an app like YNAB (You Need A Budget), Monarch, or even a simple spreadsheet in Google Sheets. Don't go crazy with categories. Use five or six buckets max: bills, groceries, gas, spending, savings, debt. Too much detail slows people down. The key is consistency, not complexity.

Now layer in automation. Set up auto-transfers to your savings account, even if it's just ten bucks a week. Schedule your debt payments the day after your paycheck hits so the money's gone before temptation shows up. Use calendar reminders for due dates, and text alerts for low balances. Automate like your future self depends on it—because they do.

Budget check-ins are your secret weapon. Once a week, sit down with your money for fifteen minutes. That's it. Don't wait for disaster. Just check in. Look at what you spent. Look at what's coming. Ask yourself one question: "Does this budget still match my life?" Adjust as needed. That rhythm turns chaos into calm. Make it part of your weekend. Put on music. Light a candle. Bribe yourself with a snack if you have to. The habit is the win.

Use triggers to your advantage. If you always spend money when you're bored, stressed, or lonely—catch that cue. Put a sticky note on your debit card: "What do I really need right now?" Add an app blocker to your phone. Create a money-safe routine when you feel triggered. One client made a rule that she had to walk around the block before any unplanned purchase. Nine times out of ten, she didn't want it by the time she got back.

Visual trackers work wonders too. Print a thermometer chart and color it in every time you knock down another $100 in debt. Move marbles from one jar to another. Put stickers on a calendar. It sounds silly—until you feel how good it is to see progress. This is how you rewire your brain to chase the long game.

Finally, make your environment support your goals. Unsubscribe from retail emails. Leave your credit card at home. Keep a reminder of your "why" in your wallet or on your mirror. When you forget what you're fighting for, you stop fighting. Keep it in your face.

You don't need to be a machine. You just need the right mix of tools and triggers that help you act like the person you're becoming. Once your systems are set, momentum takes over. You don't have to fight every day. You just have to follow the path you've built.

The right tools don't just make debt payoff easier. They make it inevitable.

Side Hustles, Windfalls, and Found Money — Supercharge Your Payoff

Sometimes, getting out of debt fast means boosting your income just long enough to break the cycle. We're not talking about working three jobs until you collapse. We're talking about temporary power moves. Quick hits of cash that go straight to your debt plan like a financial sledgehammer.

Start with the easy stuff: found money. That's anything you weren't expecting or budgeting for. Tax refunds, bonuses, birthday money, rebates, even loose change. Most people treat found money like "free" money and blow it on something shiny. Don't. Treat found money like rescue money. Funnel it straight into your next debt target. You'll be amazed how fast it adds up.

Next up: sell something. Everyone has a few hundred dollars sitting in their closet. Clothes you don't wear. Gadgets you don't use. Furniture you don't need. Post it on Facebook Marketplace, OfferUp, Craigslist—wherever. Take clear photos, write honest descriptions, and price it to move. One weekend purge can knock out a full credit card minimum payment or more.

If you're willing to hustle a bit harder, take on a small side gig—but only if it won't burn you out. Babysitting, dog walking, tutoring, Uber, food delivery, freelance writing, selling digital products, renting out a spare room—there's a hundred ways to earn a couple hundred extra a month. The key is making sure the money has a job before it hits your account. Open a separate "debt kill" account if you need to. That way the extra doesn't get absorbed into lifestyle creep.

Side income is not about replacing your main job. It's about shock payments. Every extra dollar knocks interest down. Every big chunk you throw at your balance accelerates your timeline. And the sooner you're free, the sooner you can rest.

You can also look inside your current job. Is there room for a raise, overtime, or commission? Could you pick up an extra shift once a week? Could you offer to trade flexibility for more hours short-term? Even a few hundred extra a month, directed intentionally, changes everything.

The big win here is stacking. Combine strategies. Sell your old bike. Deliver groceries three hours a week. Throw in your tax refund. Suddenly you've got $1,200 this month instead of $300. That's not just progress. That's leverage.

Remember: every dollar has power. Your plan isn't about working yourself to the bone. It's about pushing hard in strategic bursts. Give yourself a clear timeline. Maybe it's a 90-day hustle window. Maybe it's one big weekend a month. But when that money comes in, treat it like dynamite for your debt. Light it up.

You don't need a second career. You just need a short-term punch to the gut of your balance. These side wins aren't forever. But they'll help you get there faster, breathe easier, and prove to yourself that you have more power than you think.

When You Fall Off — Reset Fast, Don't Spiral

You're going to mess up. Let's just get that out of the way. You'll overspend. You'll miss a payment. You'll slip back into an old habit and wonder if you're cut out for this. That's not a maybe—it's a guarantee. But here's what matters most: what you do after the mess-up.

Most people fall off once and decide the whole plan is broken. They throw the budget out the window, ghost their bank app, and start telling themselves a story that goes something like: "I knew I'd screw this up. I'll never get it right." That story is more dangerous than any missed payment.

You don't need to be perfect to pay off debt. You need to be resilient. That means learning how to fall and get back up—fast, without drama, without shame. Think of your plan like a GPS. You take a wrong turn? It doesn't yell at you or call you a failure. It just says, "Recalculating." That's you. Recalculating. Adjusting. Moving forward.

Let's say you blow your grocery budget. You were stressed, tired, hungry, and the sale on frozen pizza was calling your name. Cool. Write it down. Log the spend. Ask, "What can I shift next week to offset this?" Then do it. No self-loathing. Just data, decisions, and a reset.

Maybe you forgot a bill. The fee hits, and your balance takes a hit. Take a breath. Call the company. Ask if they'll waive the fee—many will if it's your first miss. Set a reminder for next time. Learn the lesson, build the system, and keep moving. You didn't ruin everything. You tripped. Get up.

Sometimes the fall is emotional, not financial. You get overwhelmed. You start to feel like you'll never be debt-free, like you're working this hard and it's barely making a dent. That's real. It's valid. But feelings aren't facts. Pull out your tracker. Look at how far you've come. Even if the numbers feel small, progress is progress. Remind yourself: You're in the game. That alone is huge.

Another sneaky danger is the "I deserve it" moment. You've been doing great. You've stuck to your plan. You think, "I've earned this splurge." And maybe you have. But here's where it can derail you: when the treat turns into a trend. One reward becomes a weekend of spending becomes a month of backsliding. If you're going to reward yourself—and you should—plan it. Budget it. Make it intentional. That way it feels like a celebration, not sabotage.

And when life really hits—unexpected expenses, emergencies, layoffs—you don't quit. You pivot. Refill your emergency fund if it took a hit. Rework your plan. Maybe the 12-month timeline becomes 15. So what? You're still moving. You're still in control. Debt payoff is not a straight line. It's a messy, human, winding road. You win by staying on it.

One of the strongest people I've worked with had to restart her plan three times. Medical bills, job loss, then a divorce. Every time, she adjusted. Every time, she got back up. It took her two years longer than she hoped, but she did it. And now? No debt. No shame. Just strength and clarity. That's what matters.

When you fall off—and you will—talk to yourself like you'd talk to your best friend. You wouldn't say, "You're such an idiot, you blew it." You'd say, "Okay, you slipped. What's the next move?" Be kind. Be honest. Be relentless about coming back.

The people who get out of debt aren't the ones who never mess up. They're the ones who keep coming back after they do. Reset fast. Don't spiral. Make it boring if you have to. Mess up. Reset. Keep going.

You've got a plan now. You've got tools. You've got the truth. That's more than enough.

Fall down. Stand up. Go again.

You're still winning.

And now, you're unstoppable.

The Day It All Changes

There's going to be a day—not marked on a calendar, not circled in red—when something quietly shifts. You'll wake up, check your account, and feel different. Lighter. In control. You won't be waiting on the next paycheck like it's oxygen. You won't feel that quiet dread every time a bill hits. You'll breathe without flinching.

That's the day this work pays off. And it's coming.

Not because you're perfect. Not because you gamed the system or won the lottery. But because you showed up. Week after week. Slip after slip. Win after win. You kept showing up. You built a system that works even when you're tired. You rewrote the story you were handed. You built peace with your own two hands.

That's no small thing. That's revolution-level stuff.

This journey you're on? It doesn't end when the debt hits zero. That's just the start. Because once you prove to yourself that you can do hard things with money—you can earn more, spend smarter, save automatically, reset after setbacks—you become unshakeable. The skills you used to get out of debt are the same ones that build wealth, freedom, and choices.

And maybe, just maybe, you'll pass this power on. You'll show someone else how to fight their way out. You'll normalize talking about money without shame. You'll tell the truth about how messy and hard and worth it it all is. That ripple effect is real. You're not just changing your life. You're breaking the chain.

So when you finish this book, don't just say, "That was helpful." Say, "This is happening." Put your plan on the wall. Make your first move today. Text a friend and tell them what you're doing. Post the tracker. Say it out loud. Momentum loves noise.

And when that quiet day comes—the one where you finally feel the shift—I hope you smile to yourself. Because you'll know.

That was the day it all changed.

Because you did.

Keep going. You've got this.

And we're all rooting for you.

Call to Action

If this book gave you clarity, tools, or even just a sliver of hope—don't let it stop here. Share it. Recommend it to someone who's in the fight too. Leave a review on Amazon or wherever you bought it. Your words might be the push someone else needs to finally take control.

And if you're proud of your progress—even a single win—share it. On social, in a text, in your journal. Tag it #CrushYourDebt or whatever feels right. The world doesn't need more perfect people. It needs more people doing the real work. That's you.

Want more tools, trackers, scripts, and support? Head to [YourWebsiteHere.com]. You'll find printable payoff charts, bonus negotiation scripts, simple budget templates, and maybe even a community to back you up.

This movement grows one voice at a time. Be loud about your progress. Be proud of your fight.

You didn't just read a book. You started a comeback.

Bonus Resources

Printable Debt Thermometers – Color in your progress. Keep it visible. Make it real.

Weekly Budget Review Template – A simple one-pager to track spending, wins, and pivots.

Script Vault – Word-for-word lines to use with credit card companies, collections agents, and even banks.

Payoff Plan Builder – Plug in your numbers and build a 12-month roadmap that fits your life.

Emergency Fund Starter Kit – Steps to build your safety net while still crushing debt.

Habit Tracker – Turn your new routines into automatic wins.

Side Hustle Starter List – Quick ways to bring in extra money without burning out.

All of this—and more—is available free at [YourWebsiteHere.com].

This is just the beginning. Let's finish the job together.

Don't miss out!

Visit the website below and you can sign up to receive emails whenever Amy Sheridan publishes a new book. There's no charge and no obligation.

https://books2read.com/r/B-A-VPSTE-TMFOH

BOOKS 2 READ

Connecting independent readers to independent writers.

Did you love *How to Pay Off Debt Fast: A 12-Month Plan to Get Rid of Credit Card Debt, Pay Down Loans, and Break the Paycheck-to-Paycheck Cycle*? Then you should read *How to Stop Overthinking and Calm Your Mind: Quick Relief Techniques for Anxiety, Panic Attacks, and That Constant Dread*[1] by Jonas E. Hales!

[2]

Are you caught in a loop of worry, second-guessing, and overthinking so much your mind won't shut off? You've tried breathing apps, "just relax" advice, even journaling ... but the panic still hits, the spiral still opens, and you're left wondering if this is just how you'll live now.

How to Stop Overthinking and Calm Your Mind won't sell you a quick fix. It's not fluff, and it's not theory. It's for the person who needs real answers in real time. When your heart races, when online searching gives no relief, when you're stuck in traffic and your mind is racing — this book gives you the exact tools you can reach for.

---

1. https://books2read.com/u/3J1ADv

2. https://books2read.com/u/3J1ADv

You'll discover how to interrupt overthinking before it floods your day, how to ground yourself when your body feels detached, and how to use breathing techniques that don't make you feel more anxious. Inside are Cognitive Behavioral tools rewritten in plain language; scripts you can say when your brain won't stop; a daily routine designed for the high-anxiety life (yes, even the "I should have it together" version of you); and the one thing you need most — to feel *less broken*, and *more human*.

If you live with high-functioning anxiety, social anxiety, panic attacks, or simply the constant hum of worry in your head ... you'll find yourself here. Because this book meets you where you are, not where someone tells you you should be. It's actionable. It's honest. And it works.

www.ingramcontent.com/pod-product-compliance
Lightning Source LLC
LaVergne TN
LVHW090330210926
848480LV00004B/1363
* 9 7 9 8 2 3 2 0 0 8 6 4 2 *